STAND UP
FOR AMERICA

STAND UP FOR AMERICA

George C. Wallace

DOUBLEDAY & COMPANY, INC.
GARDEN CITY, NEW YORK
1976

ISBN 0-385-09411-6
Library of Congress Catalog Card Number 74-2521

Printed in the United States of America

First Edition

CONTENTS

STAND UP
FOR AMERICA

APPOINTMENT IN LAUREL

The primary campaign in Maryland should have closed in Frederick on May 13, 1972. We were carrying the same message that had produced such encouraging prospects for Michigan, where it was obvious that workers were fed up with the pseudoliberal philosophies of the Democratic regulars.

I hadn't varied my speeches much, because people seemed anxious to hear me hit the hard themes that had touched a popular chord in Florida, where it first became apparent that my support was much more extensive than any of the professional political analysts had imagined. I blasted federal government interference in state affairs, the asinine system of busing school children to Kingdom Come and back, legislation by court ruling, ruinous taxation and bloated bureaucracy, and loopholes in tax laws that permitted tax refuges in the big foundations.

I knew I was voicing the real grievances of the grass roots, and this conviction was reinforced when opposing candidates in both parties began to echo my views about busing and taxation. They could see that millions of Americans were in agreement with me, and it was throwing a scare into them. Even political commentators in the newspapers and on the radio and TV networks began to admit reluctantly that George Wallace was the front-runner.

It was gratifying to know we were running strong and that Michigan and Maryland primary voters would probably put me far out ahead of the field. But it had been a grueling campaign, and I was glad to see it reaching a pause. Frederick was the real windup, and every report indicated I would have little trouble coming out on top in Maryland. After Frederick, a rally was scheduled in Annapolis for the night of the fifteenth, and it was decided to add Wheaton and Laurel to the route. But this was just frosting on the cake. Frederick was the clincher.

It was a good meeting. The crowd was big, boisterous, and responsive. The usual groups of hecklers stayed on the fringes and were fairly quiet. I had had them with me all through the campaign, but I think I bothered them more than they bothered me. They were always disappointed in my speeches, because they always hoped I would say something really extreme and were frustrated when I stuck to the issues.

When the meeting ended, the Secret Service men told me there was a hostile gang waiting near the automobile. I called Cornelia over and told her to leave the hall first, alone or with someone else, so she wouldn't be recognized.

"I'll go out with you," she insisted. I tried to persuade her that there could be unpleasantness and danger, but she said firmly, "My place is with you."

We left together, through a cordon of helmeted police. There was a crowd shouting and throwing small objects—apple cores, sticks, some small stones, and bricks. Just as I was getting into the car a brick hit me in the chest—a glancing blow that caused no damage. I got in and we drove off, with the hecklers screeching invectives and obscenities.

We flew back to Montgomery that same night. The next day was Mother's Day, and I enjoyed a relaxed schedule. There were just a few political chores to attend to, and I had most of the day with my mother and mother-in-law and Cornelia, and the children. Later we went to visit Lurleen's grave.

Glen Curlee came over that night, and we had a long chat. We discussed things we had never talked about before, such as how much insurance I carried, what provisions I had made for the financial security of my family. I told Glen I had been saving in a limited way ever since I was elected judge, in 1952. It wasn't a large sum, but enough to provide for my family, for a limited time in case anything happened to me.

"Glen, you should do some systematic saving or investment," I urged.

He snorted. "There's a big difference between what you make and what I earn. I have to spend mine almost as fast as it comes in."

Glen later insisted that I must have had some premonition

about what was going to happen, because these topics had never come up before, even in our most intimate conversations. But it wasn't premonition. I think it was just part of the letdown after intensive campaigning.

The nearest thing to premonition was a dream my son George had about a week before, during the Michigan tour. He usually traveled in a separate plane, but one morning he insisted on riding with Cornelia and me. He was quite upset and explained that he dreamed that he saw a lot of people gathered around me, as though I was lying in state. The whole thing affected him so much that he didn't do his usual singing stint with his band that night.

I didn't pay too much attention to it, either then or later. For weeks I had been too busy to think about much except the campaign and the problems that kept arising in Alabama. It was like the old bombing missions in the Pacific. You were assigned a target, but you didn't really have time to worry about consequences or danger. The night before we flew a mission, there was a cruise-control plan to be carefully calculated and plotted so as to squeeze the last mile out of every gallon of limited fuel. Then, in flight, there were all those instruments staring at you out of the panels: pressure gauges, tachometers, altimeters, airspeed indicators, oil temperature gauges, cylinder head temperature gauges, the mixture control settings, fuel transfer switches—a thousand details that kept eyes and mind busy. There was no time to think about danger.

It was the same with the bombing run and the race back to base. It wasn't until later that the heavy thoughts began to run through one's mind, thoughts about what could have happened but didn't.

For years I had lived with the possibility of assassination. I had made enemies, and others had been made for me by people who had consistently and deliberately misrepresented my political and racial philosophies. To say that I was indifferent to the existence of danger would be incorrect. The eternal presence of the Secret Service agents was a constant reminder of what had happened to the late president John F. Kennedy, Senator Robert Kennedy and Reverend Martin Luther King. But events moved too fast to permit much time for morbid reflections.

With the campaign just about over, however, the thoughts that had been inhibited came to the surface. It wasn't premonition, just the normal reaction of a tired mind.

When Cornelia joined us, the conversation took a lighter turn. She knows how to turn off my darker moods. We commented on the Frederick crowd and what might have happened if the one who threw the brick had possessed more zip and accuracy with his high, hard one.

"The hecklers don't really bother me," I commented. "But I often wonder whether someone out there might try something foolish."

"George, you've been lucky for a long time," said Glen, "and I'm sure your luck will hold out one more day. That's all you need—one more day."

The repartee and relaxation helped, although I was tired of campaigning. I asked Glen why we couldn't stay right in Montgomery and call off the next day's schedule in Maryland.

"After all, if we can believe the reports, we're doing well and should carry the state," I explained. "Going to Annapolis won't affect the result—it's too late."

Glen agreed that the next day's schedule wouldn't influence the voting, but he pointed out that arrangements had already been made with the local people, and it wouldn't look good to let them down.

He was right, of course. But lethargy, not premonition, was prompting me to stay home.

A night's sleep didn't help much, because I woke up the next morning in an irritable mood—something that, fortunately for my family and friends, doesn't happen too often. We were due at the airport at 9 A.M., and when I went in to see how Cornelia was coming along, I found her talking on the telephone, her hair still uncombed.

"Who's that on the phone?" I snapped.

"It's Bobbie Jo," she explained. "They want me to appear on the Bonnie Angelo show in Washington tonight."

I almost jerked the phone out of her hand and told Bobbie Jo there would be no show—that as a matter of fact I wasn't even sure Cornelia would be going along on the trip. I handed the phone back to Cornelia and said, "If you don't hurry and get ready, I'll go off and leave you here."

It was an inexcusable performance, and I knew it, but I was

jumpy and tense. Cornelia put up with it meekly. She had often told me that I should feel free to let off steam with her, because she was the only person I didn't have to put on a front with. She insisted it was good therapy for me to unwind my tensions occasionally.

I remained uptight on the ride to the airport. We got there on time, only to find that the plane wasn't ready. There had been a mix-up. Someone had neglected to advise the crew that Wheaton and Laurel had been added to the schedule and that take-off would be at nine rather than ten. There was no one to fly the plane. Calls were made to the crew, but it would mean a delay of at least an hour.

"That will make us late at Wheaton," I said almost hopefully. "Perhaps we should just get in touch with the organizers and cancel out."

We couldn't agree on what to do, so I resigned myself to the inevitable and sat quietly while we waited for the pilots to show up. They arrived about 10 A.M. and we took off for Washington. As we were boarding, Cornelia turned to me and grinned.

"Honey, I'm sorry I made you late."

My surly mood didn't break until after we had left National Airport and were driving to Wheaton. Then I reached over and squeezed Cornelia's hand and winked at her. She smiled, and both of us recognized that the incident was over and forgotten.

There were hostile elements in the Wheaton crowd, and the Secret Service wouldn't let Cornelia go on stage as she usually did before I was introduced. Objects were flying: tomatoes, eggs, soap with nails. But apart from the hecklers it was a fine, large crowd, and I realized it would have been unfair to disappoint them. I hit all the issues hard, and the audience was responsive and friendly.

There was only one unpleasant note. The heckling group, present at all my speeches, was close to the platform, just to my right. I had faced hecklers all through the campaign and was more or less used to them. They rarely had anything new to say, and I could usually play them for laughs from the sympathetic crowds—stock quips like "I see some members of the audience are still undecided."

I asked this group, if they didn't want me, who were they for. They shouted, "McGovern! McGovern!"

They began using abusive language, about as foul as any I had ever heard in any army latrine. It was conduct I am sure a decent person like George McGovern would have repudiated.

I think what bothered me most—and saddened me—was the spectacle of a sweet-faced girl about seventeen or eighteen mounted on the shoulders of one of the messy-bearded hecklers. She wasn't really pretty, but she had a pleasant, childish face that seemed all innocence until she contorted her mouth and started spewing some of the worst obscenities I have ever heard. I glanced at her from time to time and kept thinking, "How can there be so much hate behind such a sweet-looking face?"

But all I said was, "Is that what they teach you at the college you attend?"

I remember wondering about her family, and if they knew where she was and what she was doing and the language she was using. Her accent—and that of her companions—was definitely not Maryland. Every time she shouted something especially vile, she turned to the rest of the heckling group and waited expectantly for their approving laughter. It didn't hurt me. But it saddened me.

There was someone else in the crowd at Wheaton, but I never noticed him. Photos taken show Arthur Bremer up near the front, although not among the hecklers. I probably saw his face from time to time as I glanced out over the crowd, but it meant nothing to me and I have no memory of it.

I put everything into my delivery, and the crowd roared its approval. I wound up with a slightly raspy throat, which I was sure would clear up after lunch and before the Laurel meeting.

We drove to Howard Johnson's in Laurel after the Wheaton rally broke up. Lunch turned out to be a banquet arranged by the management in a special room set apart for me and my staff and all the Secret Service personnel. A couple of the agents stayed outside, but Cornelia went out and invited them to join us. She left early, saying she wanted to go over to Montgomery Wards, just around the corner from the shopping center, to get her hair combed. She didn't get back in time, so we had to go on to the shopping center. It was a much bigger gathering than I had anticipated, in view of the improvised facilities. Again it was a good crowd—strangely enough, with no hecklers.

I was about ten minutes into my speech when my voice began

to crack. It was only momentary, and I was able to resume at almost normal pitch. Someone passed up a cup full of honey (I learned later that Cornelia had sent over to a grocery store nearby and bought it to ease my sore throat). I never did take it.

The rally ended, and I started for the car. The people in the crowd began to shout:

"We want to shake hands with the governor!"

"Come on, George, let's shake the hand of the next President!"

I turned and looked inquiringly at the Secret Service agents with me. They shook their heads. But the crowd kept shouting—friendly, good people. And there's something in me that handshaking satisfies. I like the touch of hand to hand, because I receive a pleasant sensation of confidence and force. So I waved my finger in a negative at the agents, took off my coat, handed it to one of the agents, and started back.

"Don't go, Governor," one of them told me. "It isn't wise."

"I'll be all right," I insisted. "I'll take the responsibility."

I went to the fringe of the crowd and one by one grasped the outstretched hands and listened to the words of encouragement.

"God bless you, Governor!"

"Keep telling it like it is, George!"

I nodded and thanked them. Then I heard a voice from my right.

"Hey, George, let me shake hands with you!"

I turned and started to extend my hand. Suddenly I heard five sharp reports. I spun around to the left. My knees buckled and I dropped to the ground. There was no pain, but I knew I had been hit—and hit badly. I lay on the ground as turmoil took over around and above me. I saw a circle of confused faces with helpless expressions. I tried to move my legs, but nothing happened. It was as though they didn't belong to me at all.

"This must be the end," I thought to myself. "I'll start feeling faint and pass out, and that will be the end." I thought, I will never see Cornelia and the family again.

I looked around and saw I wasn't the only one hit. There was E. C. Dothard bleeding, and so was one of the Secret Service men (Nick Zarvos). Suddenly Cornelia, whom I had seen only fleetingly since the luncheon, loomed above me and threw herself over me in a protective gesture. If there were any more bullets coming she was determined to stop them before they hit me.

She winced as she saw the wounds, then murmured, "You're going to be all right, honey. I'm going to get you out of this. I'm going to take you home and out of all this."

I wasn't too sure what she meant at the time, but her idea was to give up the whole thing—to get out of national politics and back to the safety of Montgomery.

Someone pulled Cornelia back, although it took a lot of effort. Then someone else, a doctor I suppose, put a handkerchief on the wound in my stomach to test the bleeding pattern.

One of my staff members kneeled beside me and told me, "Don't worry, Governor. You'll be all right. It's nothing. Nothing at all."

I looked at him incredulously and said, "My goodness, Emmett, you say it's nothing. You'd better take another look."

There were nine holes, because the bullets had gone through me, hitting Dothard and the agent. Pain was starting to set in as I looked up and saw a man standing beside me, pistol in one hand. He kneeled to take my pulse, and the pistol was pointing right at my head.

"Who are you?" I gasped.

"Secret Service," was the answer.

I nodded recognition. "Well, agent, I wish you'd point that gun in some other direction. I've been shot enough for one day."

The agent looked abashed and said, "Oh, my goodness!" He quickly moved the gun. He was a clean-cut young fellow, intent on protecting me, and didn't realize where his gun was pointing. The incident was picked up by the TV cameras, and I wouldn't be surprised if the tape is shown to other Secret Service agents as an example of what not to do in such circumstances.

By this time the pain was getting to me. It grew in intensity until it took all my will power to keep from screaming. I prayed, "My God, if You're going to take me, do it quick and stop this suffering."

The pain was so excruciating that I barely remember being picked up, put into the station wagon, transferred to an ambulance, and sped off. I did not lose consciousness at any time, although the pain made me oblivious to just about everything that was going on around me. I was convinced I was fatally wounded, and I was trying to be as gritty as possible to the end.

I prayed for God to spare me but if it were not his will that he not let me suffer any longer.

A collage of images rushed through my mind: Cornelia, my mother, the children, Lurleen. Then I thought of that baby-faced girl back in Wheaton.

I thought of the two Kennedys and Martin Luther King. I remember thinking how stupid it all was, how impossible that this sort of thing could happen in a country full of such fine people. Were the hate and violence of the few going to make a martyr out of me along with the others? The pain that possessed me made me sure of it.

"What a sorry way for it all to end!" was the thought that raced through my mind. There was so much left undone, so much unsaid, so much torn fabric in the country to be mended. I tried to put the pain out of my mind by thinking back, not as they say dying people do, but trying to piece together the important things that had happened to me. My thoughts turned to Clio, the town where I grew up. Strangely, the most distant memories came back in poignant clearness.

The distant memories of my life and family ran through my mind in a clear flash: Bobbie Jo and her husband; Jimbo, my only grandson; Peggy Sue; George, Jr., my only son and namesake; my little Lee—only eleven years old; my stepsons, Jim and Josh—only seven and eight; and my mother, brothers, and sisters.

I remember praying to God, "Please let me live to see them again." My mind flashed the memories of the last few lucid moments of my first wife's life when with her weak, tired voice she reminded me, "We will all meet in heaven."

CLIO AND CALOMEL

If any single, limited area of the country was typical of the rural Southland during the 1920s and early 1930s, that area was Barbour County, Alabama, which included my home town of Clio.

Barbour County was at the edge of the Black Belt—so named not because of the relatively high Negro population but because of the color of the rich, productive soil. The soil may have been rich, but Clio, like the rest of rural Alabama towns, shared generalized southern poverty. The backward economy was a holdover from the discriminatory treatment meted to the South at the end of the War between the States.

But Barbour County's spirit was at least as rich as its soil, and was a product of the Southerner's reaction to adversity. My family was neither much better nor much worse off than the rest of the nine hundred inhabitants of Clio. Work was the requisite for survival, and that meant work for every member of the family. It has been said that there are lessons in stones, and it is remarkable what a youngster can learn while he's plowing up or around stones behind a long-eared mule. It required a dogged persistence that is a good basis on which to build a life and career in just about any field of endeavor.

The family farm—now long since absorbed into large, efficient, mechanized units—was the order of the day. My father, George Corley Wallace, Sr., had turned to farming after two years at Southern University. He bought some land through the Land Bank and was trying to pay for it right up to the day he died.

He could just as well have become a doctor, like his father, George Oscar Wallace, who became almost a legend with his extensive rural practice in Clio, and later in Bakerhill, an unincorporated town about thirty miles from Clio in Barbour County.

Or perhaps he would have been more suited for a law career, if he had gone on with his education. The fact that he dropped out and turned to making a living in farming may have had something to do with my mother, whom he met while he was still in college. She was teaching music in a little school in Blue Springs.

I lost my father when I was eighteen, and looking back, I suppose it was a mistake for him to get into an occupation that required such sustained physical exertion. I remember him as a courageous man tormented almost constantly by physical afflictions. A pneumonia attack as a baby had caused the loss of one of his lungs. Later in his life, his sinus headaches became so severe that he submitted to an operation, performed with no more than local anesthetic, in which part of his skull was removed, leaving a dent in his forehead.

After buying the farmland on credit, Father and Mother moved into an old frame house in Clio, one that had been built before the turn of the century by my grandfather, Dr. Wallace. I was born in that house on August 25, 1919. The roof leaked, there was no electricity, and there were no indoor sanitary facilities. Keeping that house functional was part of the tenacious struggle that confronted my father in providing for a growing family. An old Scottish ballad says of Wallace men, "Courage be their very soul." My father, frail and sickly, possessed rare courage of soul. What he lacked in strength of body he made up in determination and vigor. Once having chosen his lot in life, he faced up to the drudgery and rawness of the unending struggle for survival.

He was typical of the solid, hard-working, God-fearing people who inhabited, and still inhabit, rural Alabama, and whose combination of faith and sinew helped to make the state strong and prosperous.

My mother, the former Mozelle Smith, came from equally sturdy stock. Born in Florida, her family had moved to Alabama early in the twentieth century. She was—and still is—an accomplished woman, with a courage that matched her husband's. Those early days were difficult, but she met them with dogged optimism rather than supine resignation. I didn't appreciate it at the time, but she worked with all her many resources to give us as full a life as was possible in a deprived atmosphere. An accomplished pianist, she continued to teach youngsters in Clio—

including a futile attempt with me. She tended the garden, kept house (no small task in view of the condition of the property), and made sure that four active children were presentable for grade school and slicked up for Sunday school.

My memories of my early childhood are understandably fuzzy. I was entered in the Clio Elementary School about 1925, and I don't recall that I ever received any distinctions there, although I am told I was a "good student." One of my memories is of riding on top of wagonloads of cotton on the way to the gins. Along with the rest of my companions in Clio, I learned to swim at Blue Springs, Pea River, and Big Creek. My swim suit (when I wore one) consisted of overalls with the legs cut off.

It was a sort of Tom Sawyer-Huck Finn type of life, with the chores mixed with the fun. I recall picking blackberries and selling them for ten cents a gallon, with the dime going to help the family income. I learned to drive an ox team in the field, and at home I helped out by shelling pecans.

More clearly than anything else (perhaps because they were more frequent) were the Sunday church sessions, at which mother played the piano. Sunday was a big day in Clio, because religion was a strong factor in the life of rural Alabama. I think my mother's optimistic disposition and my father's uncomplaining perseverance had their roots in a deep religious conviction that colored their whole outlook on life. They never regarded themselves as drudges, nor did they waste time feeling sorry for themselves and their lot. I am convinced that there was more zest for life in Mother and Father and their hard-pressed neighbors than we find today in families with three cars in the garage, a cabin cruiser in the local marina, and the wherewithal to jet from one end of the world to the other.

It is difficult, and certainly futile, to compare values. But I do often wonder at the change that has come over some American young people as a result of a generalized affluence that has in too many cases deprived them of the stimulation of struggle and challenge. A great scientist once commented on an experiment in which he helped an emperor moth to emerge from its cocoon by slitting the sides of the cocoon. The moth came out easily, but its wings were so underdeveloped it could not fly. And the scientist moralized: "It is no favor to deprive a moth or a man of the struggle that strengthens his wings."

Some youngsters today are inundated with things for which they never had to struggle. Yet I think we were more content with our little than they are today with their much. Today a paternalistic society resolves their problems for them—economic, health, emotional. But, looking back, I think we were happier with our simple, improvised games than some of today's children are with their motorbikes and pocket computers.

Not that I would ask anyone to return to those conditions. They are gone—and good riddance. But I think it is vital for our new generations to find some new challenge to the spirit to head off the defeatism that is so manifest in dropouts and cop-outs. Somewhere along the line they need—and I am confident they will find—the struggle that gives fiber to their wings and imbues them with the will to soar.

But this is a philosophical digression that is only indirectly related to Clio. In Clio we received fundamentalist theology in lieu of philosophy, and calomel treatment in place of modern child clinic service. The calomel was administered just prior to the start of the school term. It was almost a religious rite, although the consequences were anything but spiritual. Calomel was supposed to give our systems a good cleaning out—to get rid of any accumulated potentials of illness. Most of us as kids would have vastly preferred to be unwilling and unknowing hosts of disease. I have ever since maintained that any child who could survive regular flushings of calomel emerged from the experience too tough to be laid low by common assailants.

I am not sure that calomel helped to strengthen our wings, but it certainly lightened us to the point where we were sure that by flapping our arms just a little harder we could take to the air like any bird. But I suppose every generation has its martyrs to the cause of medicine. Where it was calomel in Clio, it is now an antibiotic injected in the buttock. Of the two, I much prefer the latter.

But if there was money available to buy calomel every spring, there was little cash for some of the more pleasurable features of child life. I remember my futile pining for a dollar-and-fifteen-cent cowboy suit I saw in a Sears catalog. I believe it was then that I comprehended for the first time the awful meaning of poverty.

My rare contacts with affluence were my summer visits to my

grandfather in Bakerhill. Dr. Wallace, who had endeared himself to the county by making his rounds on horseback in his earlier years, had finally achieved the ultimate in status symbols. He had a Model-T Ford, in which he chugged over the country roads, bounced across wooden bridges, and barked to a stop in front of the homes of his afflicted patients. During those summer visits I delighted in going along with him, and I especially gloried in the deep respect he enjoyed among his far-flung clientele of all ages, economic conditions, and colors. He pulled teeth with the same dexterity with which he applied a splint or made an incision in a wen. I paid little attention at the time, but an examination of his books many years later showed how rarely he was paid for his services, and when he was paid it was often as not in the form of a hen or a basket of yams.

I never knew my grandmother, the doctor's first wife, as she died four years before I was born. But I found a beloved substitute in my stepgrandmother, who married the doctor in 1919. Nora Mae Wyatt became affectionately "Mother Mae" for me, my twin brothers, and my sister.

The fact that a thirty-mile trip to Bakerhill was such a momentous event is symbolic of the relative isolation in which the inhabitants of Clio lived. The REA had still not been formed, and only a few homes were equipped with on-again-off-again electric plants. One of the highlights of my young life was the thrill of listening to the broadcast of the Dempsey-Tunney fights over C. D. Wallace's static-plagued radio. Later on, when the REA established the Pea River project, we had electricity of our own, and our own radio, with which we were edified by Lowell Thomas, amused by Amos 'n' Andy, Lum and Abner, and Fibber McGee and Molly, and entertained by Smilin' Ed McConnell. It was important, I think, because we were finally in touch with a world beyond Barbour County, and even beyond Montgomery and Birmingham.

The radio put us in closer touch with national politics, and the first presidential campaign I remember was between Hoover and Al Smith. My father, like practically all Alabamians, was a hardcore Democrat, and the state went to Al Smith. The religious issue was there and was worked for all it was worth, but Protestant Alabama voted in majority for a Catholic—just as it was to do many years later in the Kennedy campaign. It all gives rise to curious reflections, and of course belies the popular idea that Southerners are unrelenting bigots. I have often wondered why the northern states that gave the victory to Hoover never acquired the stigma of bigotry. It appears that, when judging the South and the North, people tend to use yardsticks of different lengths.

The inspiration of the Hoover-Smith contest lasted several years, and some four years later I entered politics with vim and energy at the age of thirteen. My father was supporting Fred Gibson in the primaries for secretary of state, and I was determined to help. I knocked on every door in Clio, pleading with people to vote for Gibson. Even in Gibson's loss of the state-wide race, there was satisfaction for me in the fact that he carried the town of Clio.

Wealth struck the Wallace family in 1932 in the form of an inheritance from a "rich" granduncle. Uncle Will McEachern was a traveling salesman who had managed to accumulate at his death what was then a tidy fortune. When it was divided among the heirs, my father received about five thousand dollars—an amount that in rural Alabama in 1932 was almost too vast to be encompassed by the imagination.

I'm sure there must have been considerable discussion between Father and Mother about how best to use the money. But the decision that Father finally announced met with unanimous approval: "We're going to build a house with a roof that don't leak!"

And so he did. It was a modest brick house, single story, with that marvel of marvels, an indoor flush toilet. Father was a good bargainer and acquired material at under market prices, and the house was completed for only thirty-five hundred dollars. It not only had plumbing, it had a telephone in the front room—a circumstance that, strangely enough, contributed to my boxing career as a teen-ager.

Father started it all when he bought boxing gloves for me and brothers Gerald and Jack. Father loved sports of all kinds, and since he couldn't take an active part he derived vicarious satisfaction in the exploits of his sons. The role of the telephone needs explaining. Our new home was right across the street from the Clio telephone exchange, run by John Horne. John could see right into our living room, which was set up as a boxing ring, with a single overhead light hanging from the ceiling. Timekeeper John would ring our telephone to start a round, then ring it again to signal the round's end. This would go on until we were too exhausted to continue.

Mother tried valiantly to teach me the gentler art of music, but I must have been born with a tin ear. In addition to being almost tone-deaf and having little disposition, I was subjected to the usual distractions of young boys at their hours of practice. There was nothing harder than trying to concentrate on clefs and tempos while my playmates waited impatiently outside and every couple of minutes urged me, "Aw, come on, George—stop that sissy stuff and come out and play football!"

Events finally caused Mother to realize that her teaching had been a mere prelude to disaster. It happened at a recital at the Clio-Barbour County High School. I had memorized a piece that, like most compositions, was fairly easy at the beginning and intricate toward the end. When my turn came at the recital, I breezed through the first part without missing a grace note. Then I came to a sudden, horrible stop. I had forgotten the last part. In disgust with myself, and probably in vengeance at the instrument of my humiliation, I slammed both hands down on the keys, hard, then got up and walked off—to the amusement of the audience and the deep dismay of my mother. That was the end of any dreams my mother might have had for a career as a concert pianist.

I managed to do a little better with the guitar, in spite of my tin ear. Not far from our home lived Cass Welch, a black man who could make a fiddle whine and laugh and sing. I knew the fiddle was out of my range, but Cass set out to teach me to play the guitar. I finally scraped enough money together to buy a secondhand instrument that I couldn't tune without help. The beauty of the guitar is that you don't need to have an ear, just the knack of shifting the position of the fingers at the right time. I rarely knew when it was the right time, but when Cass and I played at Clio square dances, Cass waggled the signals at me with his unlit cigar. If I was slow in shifting he'd growl, "Change!" out of the corner of his mouth. It was pretty ragged, but I don't think the square-dancers paid too much attention to the guitar lag. Cass was carrying the melody with fire and frenzy, and that's all the dancers cared about.

Cass later moved away from Clio and settled in Ozark. I used to see him frequently when I was a circuit judge, because he'd always come and sit in the court room whenever I was holding court. The unlit cigar was ever-present, and I was always half expecting him to shout, "Change!" right in the middle of a prosecution summary.

The shift from elementary to high school brought about profound changes in the pattern of my young life. Although I was never noted for scholarship, I did have a strong interest in history, especially when it touched on the Southland and gave me an insight into the area's economic and social problems that maturity was helping me to appreciate. High school also provided new outlets for physical energy and youthful spirits. I don't know what the coach thought when he saw that skinny, 120-pound freshman among the aspirants for the Barbour County High School football team, but I made up in aggressiveness what I lacked in brawn.

I wound up my senior year as quarterback and team captain, weighing an almost staggering total of 120 pounds, and we managed to compile an impressive win-loss record. Father always worried about me playing against tackles and guards who outweighed me considerably, and there were times when *I* questioned the wisdom of going out onto a field full of giants intent on knocking me down and preferably out.

My strategy as quarterback, dictated by my size, was not to attempt to do any scoring on my own, but to use my heavier companions in line plunges and try to keep the opposing team off balance by mixing plays and taking advantage of my speed and mobility. I never forgot how dependent I was on my teammates. Nor will I ever forget one hastily improvised play concocted by center Virgil Pelfry for the purpose of letting me get into the scoring during one game in which we had accumulated a comfortable lead. The plan was for Pelfry to open a big hole in center and let me scat through across the goal. He opened it wide, but before I could get scatting it closed up tight again, with Pelfry on the other side of the menacing mass. He just reached across the pile of bodies, grabbed me by my jersey, and lifted me right over the pack, depositing me across the goal line.

I was appreciative, if shaken. I picked myself up and dusted myself off and told Virgil, "If it's all right with you, let's not call that play any more."

BARBOUR BANTAM

Boxing had interested me ever since Father bought us our first set of gloves and we squared off in our front room across from the telephone exchange. I was wiry and agile, and probably too aggressive for my own good. But I thrived on the raw, face-to-face competition that boxing demands.

I got my first real mouthful of leather during the 1935 Bernarr MacFadden Tournament in Montgomery. I was a legitimate bantam at 118 pounds. I was matched against an older, more experienced boxer by the name of Tommy Denton. The first round was a disaster, as I went to the canvas twice. It was in the second round that I discovered that Denton was out of condition and had spent just about all his energy in the first round. I jabbed and hooked him almost at will for the next two rounds and won a unanimous decision.

Looking at my face after the fight, no one would have suspected that I had won. My cheeks were puffed and my eyes were purple slits. That night, on the street, a Montgomery policeman stopped me and wanted to know who had beaten me up. He was convinced somebody should be arrested.

I went on to Birmingham to the finals. I was training at the YMCA and was matched with a boxer by the name of Aaron Franklin. The night before the main bout, my coach, J. P. Hanks, told me to call off sparring and go for a walk to discuss strategy.

We walked a block or so from the Y, which was in a tough district in those days. A routine street fight broke out, and a couple of white hoodlums started to gang up on a black boy. Hanks, acting with a coach's instinct to protect a fighter, grabbed me by the arms and tried to pull me from the scene. I remember freeing myself and running to protect the hapless black boy. Others joined the melee on both sides, and there were ineffective punches thrown and an awful lot of pushing. With whoever was helping out, we managed to get the black boy free.

Hanks later insisted that I had broken my hand in that free-for-all, but my memory is that it wasn't that bad. I recall it as no worse than a sprained thumb. I went into the fight against Franklin the following night, and if the hand wasn't broken before the fight it certainly was before the first round was more than a minute old. I had to favor the hand all through the bout, and lost the decision.

I endured the pain in my hand for several days, but it kept getting worse. I was finally convinced it was more than a simple sprain and went to see a Dr. John Blue. He gave me a tongue-lashing for waiting so long and said that if I hadn't come in for treatment when I did I would probably have developed blood poisoning and lost the hand. He set it, and it was as good as new in a few weeks.

The story has since been glamorized, with embellishments contributed by Hanks. The basis of the story is true, but I must disclaim all the heroic details.

I didn't have as much trouble the following two years, winning the Alabama Golden Gloves Tournament twice in a row. I went to the regional finals in Nashville in 1936 and lost to Lester Pooley (now deceased) of Florida. In 1937, several of the Alabama Golden Gloves champions did not see action in the regional finals, as we all came down with the flu and had to default.

Boxing was a highly popular sport in the Southeastern Conference during the late '30s and early '40s, and I won a spot on the University of Alabama boxing team as a freshman. My class schedule didn't permit much training, and as a matter of fact Dean Farrar had established very strict rules about participation in athletics by law students. He insisted that students engaging in sports take a lightened course.

I had violated the rule in my freshman year and was doing the same as a junior. Boxing coach Richard E. Brickates of Saco, Maine (now deceased), told me, "George, I want you to go to the Southeastern Conference Tournament with us." I had no desire to go, because I had not trained properly and didn't want to go up against the best in my division without being in shape.

I told the coach I would go if Dean Farrar authorized it. "You know his rules," I said. "I can't afford to jeopardize my semester."

The coach agreed, and I thought I was safely off the hook. I made an appointment with Dean Farrar and put the matter squarely up to him.

"Dean," I said, "you know I fought on the boxing team last year?"

"Oh, did you?" He knew very well I had.

"Yes, sir, and I had a pretty good record. Now the team is planning to go to the Southeastern Conference Tournament in Baton Rouge and they want me to go along and fight. I told them I couldn't go because of your rule about participation in athletics. They insisted that I ask you anyhow. But I want you to know that if you don't approve, I'll abide by your ruling."

Dean Farrar didn't make any comment for a few moments. Then he said, "Let me ask you a question, Mr. Wallace. Where do you hit a man to knock him out?"

This wasn't the way I wanted things to go at all. I had expected an immediate denial. "Well, Dean, I understand that a good jolt on the jaw affects the brain enough to cause temporary unconsciousness."

"Very interesting," the dean replied. "You know, I don't believe anybody will ever whip Joe Louis." (Louis was originally from Alabama.)

"Not in his prime," I answered. "But if he keeps on fighting beyond that, someone will do it."

"Well, I tell you Joe Louis is some fighter," the dean insisted, "and I don't believe anyone will ever whip him."

I agreed. Prospects were looking worse by the moment. Then the dean asked, "How long will you have to be gone?"

I was relieved. This would settle things. "At least four days."

"Well, that's not such a long time. If you won't be gone more than four days, you go ahead down there and win that tournament for the honor and glory of the law school."

I managed to thank the dean, somewhat wryly, and headed straight for the gym to start some fierce workouts and try to get into shape. I didn't quite get into proper condition for the tournament, although I made it to the finals, losing to the intercollegiate national champion, Al Michaels (now a golf pro in Baton Rouge).

I don't really think it was resentment that caused me, after that episode, to take frequent pokes at the bust of the dean in the law school hall. It was just that he had a prominent jaw and I couldn't resist giving the statue a light left jab whenever I passed it. The practice ended one day when I was taking my usual poke at the inviting chin and heard a voice behind me. "Mr. Wallace, just what are you doing?" There was Dean Farrar standing behind me, two law books under his arm. I still don't remember what I replied, except that it wasn't very convincing.

My fighting record finally stood at twenty-five wins, four losses, and a draw—not counting the few club fights at which I picked up five or ten dollars. I liked fighting, but not enough to make a career of it.

Always on the lookout for ways to pick up money, either to help out the family or take care of personal needs, I learned that there would be openings for pages for the 1935 Alabama state legislature. I started writing to all the senators, and then I went to Montgomery and stayed there a week. I talked to all the senators I could run into, soliciting their backing.

Winning that page's election was probably the key to much of my later interest in politics. I enjoyed myself immensely, as I felt that I was a part of the legislative process. I met and observed all types of politicians from all over the state, and I got an insight into political maneuvering.

The big issue at the time, as I recall, was liquor. The legislature was divided fairly closely between the wets and the drys, with the latter holding a precarious edge. The lieutenant governor (and president of the senate) was supporting the wet interests and I admired him tremendously. I felt honored when, right before a crucial vote on the issue, he called me over and told me to go out and find a certain senator.

"He's got to be here to vote wet, so bring him in drunk or sober," were my instructions.

He gave me the name of a hotel in Montgomery where I could probably find the absentee, and I went off at once. I got to the hotel, and there in the lobby was accosted by another senator—a dry—who wanted to know what I was doing there. I told him I was looking for Senator X.

"Is there a vote coming up?" he asked me excitedly.

"Yes, sir," I replied.

He raced off for the legislature, leaving me to continue what proved to be a futile search for the missing senator.

It was a close vote, with the wets just squeezing through. And whenever he had an opportunity, the lieutenant governor reminded me in well-chosen words how close I had come to causing the majority a humiliation.

Another source of income during high school vacations and later during the summer seasons at college was magazine selling. This had a dual influence. In addition to helping to finance my schooling, it gave me an opportunity to travel out of my native Alabama. I was still in the eleventh grade when I joined a magazine-selling crew in North Carolina and Kentucky, under the direction of a former Clio resident, Elton B. Stephens, who had set up a successful business in Birmingham.

Door-to-door selling of magazine subscriptions was not the easiest task in the depression year of 1936. As often as not, we had to take payment in chickens. During my second summer, 1937, I was made crew chief and we covered North Carolina, Kentucky, Michigan, and Indiana, in a Model-T Ford.

During a stop in Glasgow, Kentucky the operators of a local wrestling hall learned that I had done a little boxing, so they matched me with the local champion. I did my training by running behind the car, and won the bout handily. I don't recall what I collected for winning, but I'm sure it wasn't more than five dollars.

Those summers were rich in experience and usually produced a couple of hundred dollars to help me through the next year of schooling. There was pathos mixed with humor, as I came in contact with an infinite variety of people in various stages of poverty or affluence. My southern accent proved an unexpected asset, and I cultivated it diligently. One lady in Benton Harbor sat in her swing and listened to my sales pitch.

"Young man, I intend to take a subscription," she told me, "but I want you to talk a little longer." So I kept on drawling to clinch the sale.

We were so close to Chicago that we wanted to see the city, so we drove there one Sunday. There were chicken crates on the back, bearing a rooster and one egg, all that was left of payment for a subscription. We must have made quite a spectacle as we drove up Michigan Boulevard in the midst of terrifying traffic. I got confused and turned the wrong way into a one-way street and had to be rescued by a policeman.

"Where you from?" he bellowed.

"Alabama."

"Well, you just turn right around and head back for Alabama before you get yourself killed. And don't come back to Chicago until you learn to drive."

It was years later that I was a special guest of the city of Chicago, including the officials of the police department, and I got a laugh out of them by relating my first brush with Chicago law enforcement.

Door-to-door salesmen run into odd situations, and I had my share of strange experiences. I remember going to a small, well-kept house and being met across a screen door by a pleasant young woman. I opened the screen door and pushed a magazine into her hands and paid no attention to her efforts to hand it back to me, as we were trained to use the trick of making the customer hold the magazine as long as possible. Once they gave it back, the sale was usually lost. Finally she said, "Here, take the magazine. I feel faint." She collapsed right there in the doorway. I went in and called to her husband, and we picked the girl up and carried her inside. When she came to, she apologized and asked, "Where were we?"

"We were talking about your subscription to the *Ladies' Home Journal.*"

"Oh, yes. I believe I'll go ahead and take it."

Her husband explained that she had just had a baby a few days before.

On another occasion I approached an elegant house in North Carolina and started my pitch. The lady of the house wasn't interested in the magazine, but she was short a servant and company was coming for dinner that night. She made me an offer. She would take five years of the *Ladies' Home Journal* if I would serve as a butler during the dinner.

A five-year subscription was a fat sale. I accepted, and I buttled as best I could that night.

Many people used to buy magazines even though they could not read; they liked to have them around for visitors to look at. That was the reason, too, for one surprise sale to a blind woman.

Others bought them just to help young men like me who were working their way through college.

At one modest house in rural Kentucky the maid answered the door. She proved to be talkative and informative, saying that the lady of the house was quite old, giving her age at eighty-seven. She wouldn't be interested in magazines, I was assured. I asked to go in and talk to the lady anyhow.

The old woman had a challenging glint in her eye as I went into the sales pitch. "I tell you what I'll do," she said finally. "I'll take a subscription if you can guess my age."

I scratched my head and said, "Well, you're older than you look. You look sixty, but you're probably about eighty-seven."

She nodded her head in surprise and took the money out of her purse for the subscription.

I couldn't let the matter stay like that. I finally confessed that her maid had tipped me off about her age.

"I don't want you to regard me as dishonest—and you can cancel the subscription, if you want to."

"No such thing. I appreciate your being honest with me. I won't cancel. As a matter of fact, I want you to extend it for an extra year."

On one occasion I chased a rooster for a woman who said she would trade him for a magazine. I finally caught the bird in a cornpatch and brought it to the woman, only to find that she had changed her mind. Obviously, all she wanted was for someone to catch the rooster for her. I was so sweaty and disgusted I just turned that old rooster loose again.

The summer following my graduation from high school, I worked with Dr. J. M. Luke and Gregsby Rush, helping them vaccinate dogs against rabies, as required by Alabama law. Rush resigned his job as inspector that fall. Needing summer work to finance my college education, I applied for the job and was accepted.

I recall that rabies was much more feared then than it is now. Under a state program, inspectors traveled through the rural counties of Alabama, checking to see if all dogs had been vaccinated and, if not, to do the job on the spot, giving the owners a certificate.

We advertised in local papers and put up signs in country stores telling the people where and when their dogs could be vaccinated. The fee was fifty cents if the vaccination was done within the prescribed time; after that it was a dollar.

I paid for my transportation, personal expenses, and the serum. The state gave me a commission for each vaccination, and I managed to clear about three hundred dollars.

It was all quite different from the classic portrayal of the dogcatcher in cartoons, and I got to know a lot of people in my home county and neighboring counties. Very often, in making spot checks, I found that unvaccinated dogs belonged to owners who didn't have money to pay the fee. Since I was on a commission, I could exercise considerable flexibility in such cases, and I never took a dog away from anyone who didn't have the money. I remember a black farmer who had three hunting dogs that needed vaccination. I knew he was too proud to accept the service without making some kind of payment, so I told him I would take three sweet potatoes. He smiled and handed me a boxful.

Quite often, I actually did have to catch a dog to vaccinate it. And when the animal was especially big and difficult, I used the Tom Sawyer approach with the local youngsters. "I bet none of you can throw that dog down," I would say, and there was always some young stalwart who came forward to help me.

The money I earned that summer, after graduating from high school, was enough to give me a start in college. I registered at the University of Alabama in Tuscaloosa and was admitted in the fall of 1937.

I arrived on the university campus with total assets of a single suit of clothes, a few shirts and socks and underclothes in a cardboard suitcase, and just a few dollars in my pocket. Those early weeks were as disheartening as they were difficult. My grades were affected by the fact that in addition to waiting on tables at the boardinghouse I was working out for the freshman boxing team.

In November I was called back to Clio. My father, whose health had been failing for many months, had finally succumbed. The family farm was still under heavy mortgage, and foreclosure was inevitable. We managed to save the home in Clio, and Mother faced up to an almost insurmountable situation by taking a job as sewing supervisor for young girls under the National Youth Administration.

Losing my father left me stunned, although I realized he had been ailing and in great pain for a long time. With typical teenage outlook, I had regarded him as an old man at forty.

With the additional help of an NYA job, I hung on by my fingernails at the university. I don't to this day know how I managed to make the boxing team in my freshman year. There came a point when I was just about ready to cut and run, but I was encouraged to stick it out by my instructors.

"Wallace," said one, "don't try to base a decision on the first six weeks. Stick to it, and you'll do better."

She was right, fortunately. I gritted my teeth and dug into my studies without relinquishing my athletic activities. It wasn't easy, but neither was it easy for the majority of my classmates, who were in an economic situation little better—and in many cases worse—than my own. It's remarkable, however, how little whining or self-pity was heard among even the hardest-pressed of the undergraduates. We economized, denied ourselves when we had to, and took as much advantage as possible of free dances and activities. For the formal dances, if I couldn't borrow a tux from Ervin Bergbauer, who was about my size, I could rent one for fifty cents.

The boarding house where I lived and worked was owned by Dr. Ralph Adams, who later became president of Troy State University. There was an arrangement whereby my eight-dollar-a-month rent was reduced by a dollar for every roomer I brought in. I remember going to Birmingham to the train station to catch kids before they got on the train and recruit them for Dr. Adams' house, usually managing to get enough to assure me free rent. By waiting on tables six hours a day, I got free meals.

Dr. Adams later used to tell people I wasn't a very good waiter—that I stepped on my apron and stuck my thumb in the soup—but he must have been satisfied with me because I kept that job during four years of my five in college.

With the exception of the blighting effect of the death of my father, I got to enjoy college life, even if it meant carrying out a grueling schedule of work and study. The NYA job that paid fifteen dollars a month and demanded fifty hours of work made me ineligible to join a fraternity. The NYA program was designed to help students who didn't have money to go to school—and if you had enough money to join a fraternity, you didn't qualify for job assistance.

At the end of each summer vacation, the one to three hundred dollars I earned selling magazines helped to tide me over another year of schooling. I kept my jobs waiting on tables and with the NYA, but there was enough free time to permit us to indulge in undergraduate devilishness. I had met and become quite close to Glen Curlee in my freshman year, and Glen turned out to be a perfect prank companion.

Despite my later differences with Judge Frank Johnson, he was my chum in college; and I still consider him a personal friend. Glen Curlee and Frank and I used to go to dances together in law school—Glen with Audrey, the girl who became his first wife; Frank with his lovely wife Ruth; and I with Virginia Herring, a girl whom I was very close to during some of my college years. I still have pictures of the six of us, taken at dances at the University of Alabama.

Frank, Glen, and I made a mischievous trio, although Glen was undoubtedly the most irrepressible. I recall a football game at which Glen had taken a drink or two, although they had no effect on him. After the game, Glen started to go out through one of the gates and was told by a policeman that he had to use another exit.

"Well, who did you boy scouts get your orders from?" asked Glen, a reference to the fact that a number of boy scouts were acting as ushers. The policeman became infuriated and arrested Glen, marching him off in full view of all his classmates. Frank and I went up to the paddy wagon, and Glen called out, "Get me a habeas corpus—no, get me two habeas corpuses."

A visiting doctor who was with us went with Frank and me to the jail, and we watched as Glen was led in. We requested that the doctor be permitted to examine Glen, but were refused. Glen made bond promptly and we went home.

His case was set for Birmingham night court, and we accompanied him. The courtroom was jammed full of drunks and petty offenders. The doctor and I were witnesses, and Frank acted as counsel, even though he was still just a law student. I testified that Glen was not under the influence of alcohol—that I thought he had been arrested for talking too much rather than drinking too much. I said I thought the policeman—a rookie—had overreacted.

On the stand, the policeman insisted that Glen's actions had been such as to indicate that he was definitely drunk. Then Frank started cross-examining.

"Isn't it a fact, officer, that you saw very few students or other persons drunk at this ball game?"

The negative has its effect, and the policeman bristled. "Of course I saw drunks. There were drunks everywhere. Hundreds of them. You had to be blind not to see them."

"Let me ask you, officer," continued Frank, "is there an ordinance in Birmingham that requires you to arrest a man who is publicly drunk?"

"Of course there is. That's why I arrested this man."

"I see," replied Frank. "And how many other arrests did you make that day, other than Mr. Curlee?"

"One."

"What for?"

"For public drunkenness."

Frank had him. "You mean the law in Birmingham says you must arrest a public drunk, and you saw several hundred drunks while you were on patrol duty, and you arrested only two—and one of them was really sober?"

Glen was found not guilty, and all of us went to a downtown hotel to celebrate. At the bar, when Glen was asked to join in a social drink, he shook his head. "I believe I'll follow George's example and pass it up."

I recall that we threw the Tri Delta sorority house into an expectant twitter for a couple of weeks. I called the sorority president, introducing myself as a Mr. George Smith of the American Tobacco Company.

"We are about to undertake a massive advertising campaign," I told her. "We are going to put up outdoor ads all over the country, featuring the prettiest girls we can find. Tri Delta headquarters has informed us that the Alabama chapter has the prettiest girls in the entire sorority, and we would like to know if they would be interested in helping out with the advertising campaign."

Then I added, "There will be modeling fees involved—probably hundreds of dollars."

The sorority president sounded excited. "I'll talk it over with the girls. Call me back tomorrow night."

I did so and was informed that there had been unanimous acceptance. "Fine," I replied. "Of course, you realize that we will need variety in dress—and in some cases it will mean posing for photos in bathing suits."

It was midwinter. "Oh, dear," said the sorority president. "The girls probably have their best dresses here, but I don't think they have bathing suits. Can you wait while they get in touch with home and have their suits sent?"

"Of course."

I called back a week later. The girls all had their gowns and their swim suits. "When will the photographer need them?" I was asked.

"We can go to work right away," I assured her. "There is just one thing you should know, however. The ads will be for snuff, and the heading will be: 'America's prettiest girls use X-Brand snuff.'"

"Mr. Smith," came the dismayed voice from the other end of the line. "I don't think there's any need to call another meeting—I'm sure our girls won't go along with a snuff ad."

In my senior year, shortly after the war broke out, Glen joined me in another hoax, this time involving his remarkable talent for imitating Franklin D. Roosevelt. It was warm, and most people in the neighborhood spent the evenings sitting on the porch. Our rooming house backed up against a street in the rear, in a thickly settled residential area. I hooked our radio up to a microphone, and while everyone was sitting and rocking on the porches, I took the microphone and made an announcement heard all down the block.

"Ladies and gentlemen, we interrupt this program to bring you an important announcement from Washington, D.C. The next voice you hear will be that of the President of the United States."

Then Glen Curlee came on with his impeccable imitation of President Roosevelt.

"My fellow Americans. Today is another sad day in the history of America. Once again has one of our major battleships been destroyed by the imperial forces of Japan."

Glen and I could hardly keep a straight face as we saw people all up and down the street fiddling with their radios and throwing up their hands in frustration when they failed to locate the broadcast.

Glen changed his inflection.

"This is the Secretary of State speaking. This is a grave day for the United States. But we ask all citizens not to lose faith, not to panic . . ."

The buzz of activity up and down the street increased, punctuated by curses as people began to ask each other, "Where is that station? I can't get it on this damned radio!"

I learned early in my career the important role emotions can play in a jury trial. While I was still a senior in law school, I asked court permission to help an elderly attorney friend of mine, Judge Beale, who had been appointed by the court to defend a man charged with murdering his wife. Permission was granted by Judge Charles Warren, now deceased.

The facts in the case were incontrovertible. The Tuscaloosa County man had placed forty sticks of dynamite under the room where his wife slept, attached and lit a sixty-foot fuse, and then went and stayed at a cheap night spot while the fuse sputtered and finally set off the dynamite, blowing his wife to bits. The defendant had given a full confession, saying he was just sick and tired of hearing his wife nag him about having another woman.

Our only object was to save the defendant from electrocution. I remember that Solicitor Gordon Davis said that if there ever was a justification for the electric chair, this was it—and he was probably right. He had declined, as I would have done in his position, a pretrial settlement for life imprisonment.

There was little to go on except a flimsy plea that the murderer's brain had been affected by advanced syphilis. The jury and the courtroom were decidedly hostile, and our chances looked slim until the man's twelve-year-old son happened to come in during a court recess. The boy, small for his age, went up to his father and hugged him, and they both started to cry.

"Judge Beale," I said, "people are not granite. Perhaps we can inject an emotional element in this case."

Judge Beale agreed, and from then on we had the boy right at the defense table with us during the whole trial. Whenever I thought the moment was opportune, I would tell the boy, "Son, your daddy is on trial, and if he is found guilty he will die in the electric chair." That's all it needed to bring tears to the boy's eyes. He would run over to his father and hug him fiercely. Then we would ask for a recess to permit the child to compose himself. (I sincerely hope I didn't cause the boy any trauma in later life, but I felt that saving his father's life justified the crude approach.)

The strategy apparently working, we abandoned the insanity plea and concentrated on an emotional appeal. "We are not asking you to give any special consideration to the defendant, because he has committed a heinous crime and deserves punishment. But we do ask your compassion for this poor, innocent lad, who has nothing in this world but his daddy."

There was more to the plea, of course, but that was the main thrust. The jury retired and was back in thirty minutes. We knew that was a good sign, because if they had decided on the death penalty it would have taken them longer to reach agreement. The defendant was given life imprisonment.

There was a sequel to the incident. The man was sent to Kilby Prison, and by 1943 or 1944 had achieved trusty status. I happened to visit the prison (I was a private in the service at the time), and he was the one who admitted me. He asked me about the possibility of letting him out on parole.

"Look, you're lucky just to be alive and be a trusty. After what you did, no one's going to agree to let you out."

"I reckon you're right," he admitted.

A few years later, when I was working in the attorney general's office in Montgomery, I saw a small item in the paper saying that this man had died in prison from an overdose of drugs he had smuggled in, taking advantage of his trusty status.

I graduated from law school in 1942 without the slightest idea what I would do next. Normally, I would have sought a connection with a law firm, but I was caught in the uncertainty of the war. At twenty-three I was almost sure to end up in the armed forces before many months passed. With a law degree I was eligible for a commission, but I decided it wasn't what I wanted. I preferred to start at the bottom.

I ended the uncertainty by signing up for the Army Air Forces cadet program. I was sworn in and told to wait until I was called.

SENTIMENTAL JOURNEY

Night missions gave long hours for deep reflection. There was no use trying to watch the scenery, because all that was visible through the windows was a black canopy with tiny pinholes of starlight. The sense of hanging motionless in space was marred only by the roar and rhythmic throb of the engines and the glow of the turbo superchargers.

We had left someplace hours before and we would arrive someplace else in a few hours, but for the moment we were suspended in time with little to entertain us but our own reveries. On such occasions I often asked myself, "What am I doing here?" And as my thoughts raced back over a complex chain of events, I was convinced that man's fate often hinges on events that are insignificant and almost meaningless at the time they occur.

I was flying, of course, and that was what I had intended to do when I signed up for aviation cadet training after graduating from the University of Alabama. But I was flying in a status and in a manner that I had never imagined, and as I looked back I realized that it was incredible that I was even alive, much less racing through the black night toward a target on the Japanese mainland.

The year 1942 was not exactly the most propitious moment for a young man to hang up an attorney's shingle, even if he had the money to rent and furnish an office. In my own case, it would have been pointless to try to enter practice, even as a junior member in an established firm, because I was mortgaged to Uncle Sam. Already sworn in as a private in the Army Air Forces Reserve, I was expecting to be called to duty any day.

The days and weeks dragged on, and no call came. But the

need for survival was acute and I had to find some kind of work to keep eating and to provide a roof over my head. I didn't have any real debts except money that I owed to the University of Alabama—and it turned out that the university could find no record of the obligation. I was still living at the boardinghouse owned by my friend Ralph W. Adams, who was already an officer in the Army. My deal with Ralph was that I was to look after the apartments and collect the rents in exchange for quarters over the garage.

This took care of a place to sleep, but eating was the next problem. I gathered up some one hundred coat hangers (which were in scarce supply in those early war years) and sold the lot of them for fifty cents. I went through all my old clothes and set aside only those that were absolutely indispensable. I sold the rest for four dollars and fifty cents. With this sizable stake, I bought a meal ticket at Paul Bailey's Cafe, which gave me a guarantee of food for a short but essential period.

I don't recall where I heard of an opening for truck drivers on state highway construction projects, but I lost no time investigating. The war was draining off drivers, and new ones had to be hired as replacements. I hastened to the state camp and applied for a job, lying outrageously about my truck-driving experience. Getting hired was no problem, but learning to drive a truck without exposing my deception was another matter. I finally made the acquaintance of a convict trusty, and on the promise of twenty-five cents out of my first paycheck he agreed to teach me how to handle a dump truck. Once I learned which levers to manipulate, I watched other drivers as they backed up under the steam shovels and simply followed their example. I put in a twelve-hour shift, from six in the morning to six at night, for the grand salary of thirty cents an hour.

I guess the good Lord felt that in my new state of munificence I was prepared for serious romance. When I walked into the Kress Drug Store to be introduced to a pert sixteen-year-old clerk, I certainly had no idea that I was being led by fate. Lurleen Burns was a cute five-foot-three at about 110 pounds, giving the appearance of a somewhat overmature child of twelve. We both seemed to realize at the start that it was the old platitude of being "meant for each other."

We starting dating regularly, both of us aware that it was for keeps. I had little to offer to make our dates interesting, but we did the best we could with an occasional movie, long sessions stretching out sodas in the drugstore, or just sitting in Lurleen's folks' parlor and talking. There wasn't much we could plan about the future, because I was still waiting for that inevitable but long-delayed call from the Air Force. We managed to live for the moment, enjoying each day to the full and not concerning ourselves too seriously about tomorrow.

In retrospect, I suppose that right from my boxing days I was probably a bad insurance risk. Not that I was accident-prone, but I certainly was plagued by minor and major afflictions. One of the minor ones occurred when asphalt fell on my right arm during my stint as a truck driver. It put an end to my driving for the moment, and I had to look for another stop-gap job. I applied for and was given a job as a tool checker at the Army Aircraft Mechanics School, with the magnificent salary of fifty cents an hour.

This permitted a slight step-up in my entertainment budget, and Lurleen and I made the most of it. By this time, the Air Force had me puzzled and edgy. I used to go into restaurants or other public places and feel that I was the center of attention because I was of military age and not in uniform. Not a few people asked me directly why I wasn't in the service, and after resisting the temptation to tell them it was none of their business, I usually made the stock explanation: "I am in the service. I've already been sworn in and am just waiting to be called up." Sometimes I was believed; other times, I'm sure, I wasn't.

The "hurry up and wait" process for which the military is so justly famous finally caught up with me. It all happened with bewildering suddenness. It was on February 2 or 3 of 1943 that my induction orders finally arrived, instructing me to report to Miami Beach on February 1. Here I was AWOL even before starting my military career. I had frantic visions about being picked up and court-martialed.

I called Lurleen at once, then started packing my few belongings. I hailed a cab, passed to pick up Lurleen, and the two of us headed for the Tuscaloosa depot from which I could catch the "Doodlebug" to Montgomery. We arrived at the station to find the train had pulled out just a few minutes earlier. Again investing hard-earned money in a taxi, we raced down the highway that paralleled the railroad tracks and finally caught up with and passed the "Doodlebug." I got out and flagged the train down, and after a fleeting kiss for Lurleen climbed aboard and set out for Montgomery, while Lurleen returned to Tuscaloosa in the taxi.

My anxiety was dispelled on the train ride from Montgomery to Miami Beach, as I found that scores of other young recruits were as late as or later than I was—that delayed orders were nothing unusual. It was hot when we arrived in Miami Beach and were installed in a beachfront hotel that had been converted into a basic training center.

I doubt if any soldier ever had anything good to say about basic training—and even being in a Miami Beach hotel didn't improve matters much. But I continued there the process I had begun in the university, that of making friends, of mixing with young men from all parts of the country, North, East, South, and West. This wartime intermingling was a valuable unifying device for the nation, and I believe it helped in achieving better understanding and breaking down barriers and misconceptions. I must confess to a bit of malicious mischief in this respect, as my southern companions and I loved to bait some of the northern boys who had outrageous ideas about the South and its inhabitants. My fellow "rednecks" and I used to spend off-duty hours spinning the most impossible tales to wide-eyed and gullible youngsters from Chicago or Denver. I told them all about my adventures as a moonshiner in Alabama, although I doubt that I had ever met one. One of my favorite methods of ribbing my northern buddies was to get them into an argument about the heat of the sun and its influence on the earth. I took the stand that the higher one went the hotter it got, "because the sun is a ball of fire, and any fool knows that the closer you get to a ball of fire the hotter it is." I managed to convince a good many of them, and even the ones who knew instinctively that I was wrong couldn't find the right arguments to refute the thesis. And I gloated that people in the North loved to talk about the educational deficiencies of the South, yet these young men were living evidence that northern educational systems left a lot to be desired. One of my Colorado buddies went into a state of frantic perplexity when I challenged him to explain why there was snow on mountains in the West, inasmuch as the mountaintops were closer to the hot sun than were the valleys. This practical demonstration of the art of confounding helped to convince me that I had not been amiss in selecting a law career.

On the not-always-accurate theory that anyplace is better than where you are in the Army, we were all eager to ship out of Miami Beach. Basic training finally ended, and I was placed on a train destined for Arkadelphia, Arkansas, to the Quachita College campus, for college training in preparation for entering the cadet program. Apparently, cadets had been arriving at preflight bases with deficiencies in such basic subjects as math and physics, so the idea was to give them all a crash course that would help them to make the grade in flight school. The highlight of the college training program was ten hours of flight training in a Piper Cub—my first time in the air.

During all this time, Lurleen and I were exchanging letters every day. We made no telephone calls, because these were too expensive.

My hazard-proneness hit me again in Arkadelphia. I woke up one morning with a fever; there were red spots all over my body, and I started vomiting. After there was nothing left to vomit, I couldn't stop dry retching. My neck became stiff and I started to have agonizing headaches. I went on sick call and all I could tell the doctor was that I had never felt so sick in all my life. I lost consciousness soon after and woke up six days later in the Army-Navy Hospital in Hot Springs. The diagnosis was spinal meningitis, and the prognosis was gloomy.

By all counts, I should have died—or at least been left a helpless invalid. But surprisingly enough I started to recover, and the only apparent aftereffects were prolonged weakness and the loss of pounds of flesh that I didn't have to spare to begin with. I was given a recuperation furlough and took the first train back to Tuscaloosa.

My reunion with Lurleen confirmed what both of us had long known—that we were desperately in love. We wanted each other so much that we decided on immediate marriage, overlooking such irrelevant details as practically no income and the fact that I was a private in the Army and would be bouncing around from nowhere to elsewhere for the rest of the war.

Lurleen was working in a photo studio at the time, but she

was as decided as I was. I remembered a Jewish justice of the peace that I had been good friends with when I was a student in Tuscaloosa. Judge Adolph Forster had a physical handicap and lived in his office. I wanted Judge Forster to get the fee for performing the ceremony, and after overcoming the legal obstacle of Lurleen's tender age by having her mother's written consent, and forcing Judge Forster to take the enormous fee of one dollar, Lurleen and I were married on May 21, 1943.

We had our marriage banquet with Lurleen's mother, Mrs. Henry Burns, then took the "Doodlebug" to Montgomery to see my own mother, who was working in the state capital as a secretary. After receiving Mother's blessing—given somewhat in awe when she saw the young thing her son had taken to wife—we decided to make the family rounds and headed for Clio. On the way, we stopped off at Brundige to visit my great-aunt, Mrs. Hadley McEachern. Aunt Hadley was a sort of challenge to me. In all the history of the Wallace family, she had never been known to approve of a single marriage match. She met us at the door, limping as a consequence of an earlier stroke, and came out with her stock phrase: "Lord have mercy, I'm glad to see you."

I don't know exactly how it happened, but I really wasn't greatly surprised when Aunt Hadley broke her long tradition after just a few minutes of chatting with Lurleen. She turned to me and nodded vigorously and said, "George, you're a Wallace with sense. You've married the sweetest and prettiest girl I have ever met."*

We continued on to Clio, then to Clayton, where Lurleen completely won over my grandfather and Mother Mae.

The furlough ended, and I put up no objection when Lurleen suggested going to Arkadelphia with me. I never realized at the time just how much of a sacrifice she was making in adopting the vagabond life she was to lead for the next several months. We got a foretaste of the problems we would face when we started looking for quarters for her in Arkadelphia. We finally found her a room with Mrs. "Mom" Sanders, who had already become a

* I was on duty in the Pacific when I received the news of Aunt Hadley's death, and the fact that there was a bequest of one thousand dollars for me in her will. This money helped to give me a start after the war ended and I went back to Alabama.

living legend in Arkadelphia because of her dedication to being a house mother to servicemen and their wives.†

I had to live on the college campus, of course, and was allowed out only on weekends. During the week, however, Lurleen could come onto the campus after my duties were over, and we used to stroll around the lovely grounds until it was time for her to go back to Mrs. Sanders' boardinghouse. The school auditorium had been converted into a barracks, and it had a single telephone. I lined up every night and took my turn, and Lurleen always sat up waiting for my call, even though we had been with each other just a few hours before.

My stay at Quachita came to an end with my transfer to San Antonio Aviation Cadet Center–known then as SAACC–and Lurleen had to go back to Mobile, where her father was employed in a defense plant. At San Antonio I received my first disappointment as a soldier: I was informed that the bout with spinal meningitis had left me physically disqualified to continue in the cadet program. I was, to use the then current term, "washed out."

From San Antonio I was sent to Amarillo, a training center for multiengine airplane mechanics. I was assigned at first to the orderly room before being sent out to Lincoln, Nebraska, where there was a single-engine mechanics school. I was about to start looking for a place for Lurleen to stay in Lincoln when I was bounced right back to Amarillo, to go to multiple-engine mechanics school.

Lurleen joined me just as soon as she could, and once more we went through the tortuous process of finding a place to live. We finally located a five-dollar-a-week room (with a cloth door) in a house owned by Mrs. Catherine Thiedens. Mrs. Thiedens turned out to be a wonderfully sweet person who delighted in driving us around in her car on Sundays, shaking off all my offers to do

† "Mom" Sanders used to write to all the boys telling what all the rest were doing. When I was inaugurated as governor of Alabama, the citizens of Arkadelphia raised money to send "Mom" Sanders to the ceremony. She also came to Lurleen's funeral. "Mom" died while I was in the middle of the presidential campaign, and I attended her funeral in Arkadelphia—along with numerous other ex-servicemen for whom she had been a loving house mother. I was asked to speak a brief eulogy, but I was so choked up I couldn't: "Mom" was one of my last strong links to Lurleen.

the driving. We had a hot plate in the room, and Lurleen did the washing in the bathtub.

My work at the base meant getting up at four-thirty in the morning to catch a ride in with a buddy who owned a car. I was still on private's pay, but I managed to make a little extra on my days off by working in the Pantex Ordnance Works, loading five-hundred-pound bomb casings and storing TNT in "igloos." They needed help so badly I could put in a few hours on weekdays after finishing my shift at the air base. In addition, I mowed the landlady's lawn once a week for a dollar.

Lurleen was also working, at a twelve-dollar-a-week job in a local five-and-ten. We used to buy old potatoes in the corner store because they were cheaper. We went to an occasional movie, but mostly we did a lot of walking. It was a Spartan life, but there was no complaining on either side; we were determined not to let the problems of mere living get us down.

My previous service in the orderly room at the Amarillo base helped make my period of mechanics training more pleasant than it was for most of the other students. There was an arrangement with the top sergeant, Sergeant Duncan, as tough a soldier as he was staunch as a friend. During inspection line-ups, he used me as the squadron scapegoat, chewing me out unmercifully because I hadn't shaved close enough, or because my clothes were not as neat as they could be, or because he couldn't see his reflection in my boot tips. The other students commiserated greatly with me for being picked on so unjustly, completely unaware that this was just the top kick's method of putting the fear of the Air Force into the rest of them. My reward consisted of overnight passes to stay in town. On one occasion, Sergeant Duncan called me out of formation and ordered me to do a rightabout-face. I messed it up, and my feet ended up about a foot apart after making the turn. Sergeant Duncan immediately entered into a doleful lecture about the sad state of the United States Army Air Forces, which were obviously scraping the bottom of the barrel to get their sad-sack soldiers.

I took my mechanics training seriously because I realized that the lives of the crews depended on how well the planes were maintained. After graduating from mechanics school, I worked awhile on the line at Amarillo, then went into the first phase of flight-engineer training.

The whole thrust of the flight-engineer program was the increasing use of B-29s in the Pacific theater. The Boeing giant was already being used on a limited scale in the Chinese and Burmese areas, but it was so big and complex in its operation that it needed a flying mechanic in addition to the pilot and copilot. Hence the stepped-up demand for flight engineers.

During this training period, Lurleen had become pregnant and went back to live with her parents in Mobile. She was back in Amarillo in a week and remained until shortly before her delivery time arrived. By that time, I had completed the flight-engineer mechanics training and was in Lowry Field in Denver for advanced courses in cruise control. There I learned of the birth of our first child, Bobbie Jo, and tried to get a furlough. I was turned down, on the perfectly reasonable grounds that if every new father in the Army went home for a birth, the Army would be half depleted at almost all times.

From Denver I went to Alamogordo for more training. Some of the flight engineers on B-29s were given commissions, but most of us were either sergeants or warrant officers. I was the former. It was perfectly all right with me, for several reasons: I felt that I could serve my country just as well as an engineer as I could if I had gone into Officer Candidate School and come out as a ninety-day-wonder shavetail. And there was also some political intuition in back of my reluctance to go into officer training, for which my college education qualified me. I sensed that if I got back to Alabama and into politics, there would be far more GIs among the electorate than officers. That this intuition was sound was proved in my first campaign for the legislature, in which one of my opponents was a former army officer, and I was elected by the votes of former enlisted men who didn't know much about me except that I had been an enlisted man myself.

I met my daughter for the first time, in Alamogordo, in early 1945. Lurleen had traveled in a second-class coach all the way from Mobile, but that was nothing compared with the martyrdom she faced on arrival in a town that had no spare living quarters. We hunted all over the town and finally found a room, only to be forced to give it up when the landlady's soldier son returned home.

Once more scouring the town, we finally found a family that let us sleep on a screened porch for a single night. For the next several nights, we settled for a single room in which we had to use a dresser drawer as a bed for the baby, Kayo Mullins style.

Lurleen was as usual sweet and uncomplaining, but I was disgusted with myself at not being able to provide her with a decent home. Fortunately, we were able to graduate from these lavish quarters a few days later to acquire the luxury of a chicken house. A man named Barnwell, who owned the property next door, had just finished converting an old chicken house into living quarters. We took one look and snapped it up. It was clean, although not too roomy, and it had a gas hot plate. We took Bobbie Jo out of the dresser drawer and moved into the chicken house, where we lived in relative comfort until I was once more transferred.

This time, we traveled together back to Mobile, as one of the incentives of going to Alamogordo had been the promise of a furlough before moving on to Topeka to join my plane and crew. It was a long, tedious trip on a crowded train. The baby cried, as babies will, and I had to try not to listen to comments of the rest of the occupants of the coach when they awakened from a midnight doze and snorted, "Who does that damned baby belong to?" The train had a diner, but dining-car prices then as always were out of reach of our budget; we bought sandwiches and soft drinks from vendors.

The furlough in Mobile had that extra poignancy that came from a realization that it could be our last time together. After Topeka, it was to be the South Pacific, and there was no assurance that we would be able to see each other before I left. Then there was the other possibility that neither Lurleen nor I discussed but was in the back of our thoughts at all times. Some of the crews that had trained ahead of me in Alamogordo had already gone into action in the Pacific, and we had received word of casualties. I tried to maintain my composure when I said good-by to Lurleen, but as I walked down the steps with my flight bag a feeling came over me that I might never see her again. I broke down and cried for the first time as a man.

The stay in Topeka was brief, just long enough to become acquainted with the other crew members and take orientation flights with our new plane, named by unanimous consent *Sentimental Journey*. I obtained an overnight pass while in Topeka, called Lurleen and arranged for us to meet in Memphis—the last time we were to see each other before I went overseas. My old friend Captain Ralph Adams was stationed in Memphis, and he put up Lurleen and the baby and me until I had to catch the train back to Topeka. It was another moist-eye departure.

Our crew developed congeniality right from the start. Our pilot, Captain Robert Ray, was a twenty-four- or twenty-five-year-old veteran, and the copilot was Lieutenant Jason Riley. The rest of the crew was made up of bombardier George Harbinson, navigator Robert Lamb, radio operator Dick Zind, radar operator Emil Kott, and gunners Robert Bushhouse, Arthur Feiner, Johnny Petroff, and George Leahy.

We were all impressed with the beauty and size of our B-29, and I remember wondering how that huge machine ever managed to get off the ground. As flight engineer, I was responsible for all the engine controls: speed settings, mixture controls, cowl flaps, turbos. The engineer rode backward, facing a huge panel cluttered with instruments and dials, usually in clusters of four, toggle switches to turn systems on or off, control switches for the hydraulic and electric systems, cabin pressurization, and fuel transfer. The plane was designed for the huge distances of the Pacific, with a fuel load of some forty-two thousand pounds. One of the engineer's responsibilities was to preplot fuel consumption and make the necessary mixture and power adjustments in flight to assure that the bomber would reach its target without going beyond the "point of no return." It was an awesome responsibility, and I was already beginning to have second thoughts about flying, especially in a new plane that admittedly still had a few annoying quirks. Mishaps and even deaths in the training process had been frequent enough to make all of us cautious.

But ours was a good plane and a good crew, and we went through the training period in high spirits, taking long flights over the entire Midwest, to California, to the Canadian and Mexican borders.

The meningitis that had scuttled my cadet career once again cast its long shadow in the path of flying. The B-29s were to be used in one area only: the Pacific. Health conditions in the area were such that bouts with malaria and other tropical diseases were normal and expected. The chances of exposure were greater and the consequences more severe if a soldier was already in a run-down condition. The specifications were rigid: one had to reach a certain minimum weight for his height, or he was disqualified.

At my final check in the flight surgeon's office, I was fully aware that I couldn't possibly make the weight, and the Air Force was strict about "fighting out of one's division." The scales confirmed my fears. I was given an opportunity for a recheck later that same day. I was determined not to wash out a second time, so I went to the base gym and started to drink water. I drank all I could hold, then I sat down; then I got up and drank more water and sat down again. I kept this up for what seemed an eternity, going to the bathroom when I could no longer deny my bladder. I waddled back to the flight surgeon's office and, with pain in my groin, asked to be given a recheck on the scales. The medical orderly, a sergeant, took one look at me and poked me in the stomach. "You've been guzzling water," he stated. "But go ahead, get on the scales."

The water did it. I reached the exact minimum to qualify and raced as fast as I could to the bathroom to relieve my agony.

We were finally ready for action and took off for the long flight, first to Mather Field, then to Hawaii, to Kwajalein, to Saipan, and finally to our base on Tinian, where we were assigned to the 58th Wing of the 20th Air Force, under command of General Curtis LeMay, who was later to be my vice-presidential running mate. The first week was spent flying training missions with other crews to become familiar with operational procedures. I was later involved in eight or ten raids over the mainland of Japan and a few practice raids over some of the islands. The B-29 was a high-altitude bomber, but most of our missions were made at night at altitudes of from eight to ten thousand feet. Under those conditions, anti-aircraft fire was not regarded as too effective, but when anybody is shooting at you, there is always a chance of getting hit, and we saw a number of our fellow crews and planes go down.

I flew all my assigned missions, and volunteered for at least one mission to replace an engineer who was incapacitated. My object was to complete my thirty-five missions and get back to the States.

On my first mission over Japan, flying as an observer with an experienced crew, I was assigned the task of jamming Japanese radar. At a signal from the pilot over the interphone, I was to start throwing out rolls of tinfoil, counting to ten between succeeding jettisons. The scuttling of tinfoil was supposed to stop after the bombing run was over, but there was no order from the pilot, so I just kept on throwing tinfoil into space. It wasn't until I had gotten rid of our entire supply that I discovered that my headset had become disconnected and the pilot had given the "stop" order long before.

Tinian was just one of many Pacific bases within B-29 bombing range of Japan. After completion of practice missions at Truk, our crew joined in day and night strikes at Japanese cities. The daylight missions meant a midnight takeoff from Tinian, a rendezvous over the coast just after daybreak with scores of other B-29s, then formation flying to the assigned target.

There was a vast difference between night and day bombing procedures. During the former, we flew alone and dropped bombs more or less indiscriminately on reaching the target zone. As the main object was to complete the bombing assignment, our gunners did no shooting unless we were under direct attack, as nighttime machine-gun fire would give away our position. Usually, our defense procedure consisted of evasive action.

On daylight missions, however, we flew in large V-shaped formations, depending for protection on the combined firepower of the airplanes. It was absolutely essential to stay in position, as lone planes were sitting ducks for Japanese pursuit craft. As we zeroed in on the target city, enemy antiaircraft batteries sent up intensified fire, and as I turned anxiously in my seat I could see the tense, sweating face of our pilot as he fought to hold the huge plane on course in spite of jolts of bursting flak around us.

Once the bombs were released, the formations made slow turns and headed for the coast, where we dispersed and began the long flight back to our respective bases.

It was an awe-inspiring sight as all those silver-blue-streaked planes converged in the early-morning sunlight. It was especially impressive when one stopped to reflect that the gathering armada was made up of complex and costly aircraft under the control of young men averaging no more than twenty-five years of age. I did my share of musing about why we had to fight a war with a country that diplomacy could have made our friend—and that in fact did become our staunch ally after the war. Even then, I was convinced that the greatest threat after the war would be Soviet communism.

Sentimental Journey had her close calls. On one run over the city of Osaka, smoke from the bombed area was rising higher than our plane, creating a tremendous updraft. We flew directly into the thermal, pursued by a Japanese fighter plane. All at once we were lifted straight upward, and we could see the wings buckle under the strain. The twin-engine fighter on our tail had not fired, nor had we, and when we went through the updraft the smaller plane was tossed like a matchbox. The pilot had to bail out, and we watched as he approached the ground in his parachute. Amazingly, tracer bullets were fired at him from the ground, and the last we saw of him was when his parachute collapsed, on fire.

In August 1945, we were assigned a mission to bomb a coastal city. As we approached land under the light of a full moon, we could see a glowing haze showing that the city had already been hit by pathfinders. This was to be the biggest bombing effort of the war in terms of number of participating planes and total bomb tonnage.

Just as we reached the coastline, our pilot announced over the intercom that No. 2 engine was on fire. One of the cylinders had blown and we had an oil fire from the blown cylinder. The pilot feathered the props and jettisoned our bomb load, and I immediately went through the engineer's emergency procedures, shutting off fuel controls and ignition. I actuated the fire extinguishers, which enveloped the burning engine in a carbon-dioxide foam designed to smother the fire.

The pilot gave the bail-out alert and nosed the plane down to pick up speed and help blow out the fire. I checked my parachute and the C-1 vest that contained cans of water, fishhooks, shark repellent, sea dye, etc. We were all ready to bail out at the pilot's signal.

Fortunately, it wasn't necessary. The combination of foam and airspeed put the fire out. We leveled off and headed out to sea. For a time we considered the possibility of landing at Iwo Jima, between Japan and our own base at Tinian. But after making calculations about our fuel supply and rate of consumption, we decided we could make it to our home base (curiously, fuel consumption is higher when flying on three engines than on four).

One of the reasons we decided not to land at Iwo Jima was that other damaged aircraft were stacked up in the landing pattern. Most were worse off than we were—in some cases struggling on just two engines. We made our landing at Tinian without incident, although we were chagrined at being the only plane in our bomb group to abort the mission.

Strange things happened up there in the black of night. I remember receiving a report over the headset that our gunners had picked up the lights of an unidentified aircraft following us. They trained their .50-caliber guns on the object, which they insisted was "blinking at us." We blinked back a dare to the enemy to close in and get it over with. After nothing happened for a couple of hours and the blinking light was still following us, the pilot began to wonder how it was possible for an enemy plane to get so far out of range of its home base. He sent the navigator back to see what was happening, and I could imagine the sheepish expressions on the faces of the gunners when Lieutenant Lamb announced that they had been tracking the planet Venus.

All of us swore silence about the incident. But at breakfast the next morning, we discovered that several other crews had had the same experience. I have often wondered just how many machine guns had been trained on unsuspecting Venus that night.

My last mission was flown the day before the first atomic bomb was dropped. It was a twenty-hour haul, out and back, and when we landed and went to the PX for a snack we heard that another plane from our wing group had just dropped an unusual bomb over Hiroshima. The next morning, we found orders instructing us to return to the States for lead crew training. This was specialized training for day formation flying, in contrast with night missions, which (as noted earlier) were usually solo operations. Our crew was chosen to conduct this training because of our good record of reaching primary targets (only once had we been forced to abort a mission and jettison our bombs in sight of the Japanese mainland and scurry back to base).

The new assignment would get us back to the States for from four to six weeks. On the flight to Hawaii we heard over the radio about the dropping of the second bomb, on Nagasaki, and by the time we landed in California the was was over and preparations were being completed for accepting Japan's surrender.

I received leave on arrival in Los Angeles and took the first train (not plane) for Mobile. The war came to an end officially on August 14, and in Mobile, as in all the rest of the United States, there was a wild celebration, which neither Lurleen nor I joined. I had survived the war and I wasn't going to get run over in a victory celebration.

My orders were to report back to Muroc Dry Lake, in the Mojave Desert, on August 29. I had fully expected to learn that the crew-leader training project had been canceled and was surprised and considerably disappointed to learn that the orders were still valid.

I then made a very practical, if unheroic, decision. I resolved to do no more flying. I rationalized it then, and I have rationalized it since, and I have found nothing basically wrong with the decision.

The war was over. It seemed to me pointless to embark upon a training program that would have no useful purpose and could in fact be the cause of senseless accidents. B-29 flight crews were now a glut on the market, and they were being separated from the service so fast that finance officers all over the country were wondering where all the necessary mustering-out money would come from. If there was any more necessary work to do in the Pacific with the big bombers, there were thousands of fresh trainees who could be sent in place of those who had already seen combat duty.

I felt I had done my part—nothing outstanding, but more than it would have been necessary for me to do. I could have used my physical condition to obtain a soft spot in limited service, but I hadn't wanted it that way. I could have accepted the Air Force's decision that I was too underweight to qualify for Pacific duty, but I had fudged in order to pass the test. I had no pretensions about being a hero, but I certainly had not shied away from what I felt was my duty to my country.

Now I was as weary of spirit as of body. I was still underweight and still under the lingering effects of that siege with meningitis. I had developed what today would be called a "thing" about flying. With the war ended, I found no sense in forcing myself to participate in flights that no longer served any real function.

There had been tragic and—as I was convinced—absolutely unnecessary accidents in the lead crew training program. It was a risk I didn't feel anyone should be obliged to take. Call it fear, call it anxiety coming to the surface, call it what you will—I decided I was through flying. And my stubbornness in sticking to the decision would have done credit to my Scottish forebears. An attitude such as mine, adopted by people one dislikes, is called pigheadedness; when adopted by people one admires, it becomes tenacity of purpose. But it's all the same thing: a firm and irrevocable decision and a full willingness to accept the consequences.

I announced my decision to my wing commander, and he shook his head. "I'm sorry, Sergeant, but the lead crew training program is still on. Your orders are to take part with your crew."

There was only one more recourse. I received permission to see the base operations officer, to whom I explained my reasons for not wanting to fly. There is an old saying in the Air Force that a man can't be forced to fly if he doesn't want to, but he can certainly be made to wish he had wanted to. The operations officer refused to give my request the slightest consideration. I continued, telling him respectfully that I had never been a goof-off or a troublemaker, as my record proved, that I could long ago have used my physical condition as an excuse not to be placed on flying status, that I felt I had served my country to the degree necessary, that I was no longer needed and all I wanted was a clean record and an honorable discharge.

The colonel fumed and exploded. "Sergeant, you are obviously a sick man—which is the kindest description I can make of you. I am ordering you to report to the hospital for rest and recuperation. I am ordering you to leave for the hospital this minute, and I'm going to call the hospital in a few minutes and if I find you have not reported immediately I'll see that you are court-martialed—and I'll throw the book at you."

I did as I was told and reported to the hospital (arriving only a few minutes before the base operations officer's verifying call). The doctors looked me over, and from their reaction I learned that I was in much worse condition physically and mentally than I had imagined. They found me gaunt and haggard and tense with anxiety. I was hospitalized and put on a special diet and given vitamin shots.

My crew members used to come in to see me. "We're not interested especially in you," they quipped, "but, you see, we've got bets going about whether you will be forced to fly, or whether you beat the system."

I beat the system. The rest did wonders for me, and I was finally released heavier and with almost no trace of the state of tension. By this time, there was no insistence on putting me back on flying status, and I was sent to El Paso to be discharged.

In El Paso, my papers and a fair amount of mustering-out pay in my hands, I set off not by swift commercial airliner but by a slow-chugging train to join Lurleen in Mobile. (It was a long time before I ventured to fly, although in recent years I have done so frequently and extensively.) The days of frantic dashing to take advantage of precious hours were over. I had a lot of things that needed thinking out very carefully, and the train ride would provide a good opportunity.

Above all, I made a firm resolve that never again would Lurleen have to live in a chicken house.

YEARS OF JUDGMENT

. . . if the policy of the government . . . is to be irrevocably fixed by decisions of the Supreme Court . . . the people will have ceased to be their own rulers, having to that extent practically resigned their government into the hands of that eminent tribunal. —Abraham Lincoln.

The war was behind me, and I was free to pick up the threads of my life so sharply severed by war service. It was good to know that there would be no more tearful farewells in railroad stations, or anxious and painful separations between furloughs. We were looking ahead to being a real family, almost for the first time. I still marvel at Lurleen's courage during the months and years of ordeal.

After resting a few weeks at my in-laws' home on Blakely Island, near Mobile, I decided it was time to look for a job. Wearing my khaki uniform, I left early one morning to hitchhike the two hundred miles to Montgomery. Old Highway 31 was narrow and winding, and the trip took most of the day. I went directly to Mrs. Metcalf's boardinghouse, where I had lived when I was a page in the legislature. The following morning, my morale fortified by a big southern breakfast of eggs, grits, and bacon, I left to see Governor Sparks to seek his help in finding a job.

The governor was glad to see me and remembered that I had worked hard for his election while I was still a law student at the University of Alabama. I had traveled throughout the county making speeches in his behalf. During the war he had written to me, offering to help me find work after the war was over. I used to show the worn and faded letter to my buddies, with ill-concealed pride. I realize now a letter from a governor can very well be mere form. Fortunately for me, Governor Sparks didn't regard it that way. He went to bat for me with Billy McQueen, who was attorney general for the state of Alabama.

I was a skinny ex-sergeant and looked younger than my twenty-six years; I doubt if I made much of an impression in my ill-fitting uniform. I told McQueen I was applying for the job of assistant attorney general and that I was anxious to start immediately. I was assured that my application and my military service would be taken into consideration. I couldn't understand why I wasn't hired on the spot, as the job was vacant and I was the only applicant. I went back to see Governor Sparks, and he telephoned McQueen. I was hired a few hours later at a starting salary of $175 a month.

It was a small office, and I was given letters from various state officials requesting legal interpretations. At first, I was apprehensive about my ability to write interpretations that would be acceptable to the attorney general, but after a little work and practice I acquired competence. I prepared briefs for the state in criminal cases in which the defendants filed appeals. The attorney general's office handled all appeals brought before the Criminal Court of Appeals and the State Supreme Court.

In all but a few cases, my appeal briefs for the state were upheld by the higher courts—largely because the cases had been well tried in the lower courts, not because of the brilliance of my arguments.

Not long ago, I reread some of those old briefs and was pleasantly surprised to see that they had been thoroughly researched and well written. I doubt that I could do anywhere near as well today; in fact, I wouldn't even try, as the hard detail work is now delegated to my aides in the legal department. Looking back on that apprenticeship, however, that opportunity to work and study in the attorney general's office was excellent preparation for future clashes with the all-powerful federal judiciary.

When Lurleen joined me in Montgomery, we once more faced the old problem of finding a place to live. As I recall, we stayed the first few nights at Mrs. Katie Metcalf's boardinghouse. Housing within my means was scarce in Montgomery, but we finally found a Mrs. Guthrie, who was willing to rent us a room with kitchen privileges in her small house in the Capitol Heights district. A bed and a dresser just barely fit, and after we added a baby it was no small feat to move around.

With the approach of the primaries for the state legislature, I took a leave of absence from the attorney general's office and entered the campaign, seeking one of the Barbour County seats in the House of Representatives. Lurleen was accustomed by now to our frequent moves and packed our few belongings. We returned to Clayton, moving into a house owned by Mrs. Sammy Davis.

I conducted a vigorous door-to-door, farm-to-farm campaign, with Lurleen handling the letter mailing. Although she was my most enthusiastic supporter, she was still under voting age, and I often kidded her about the theoretical chance of losing by one vote.

I had seen enough of politics to be wary of overconfidence; too many unexpected things can happen. I prefer the underdog role to that of the front-runner, who is too likely to trip over his own complacency.

There is no comparison between campaigning at the grass-roots level and the super campaigns on the national scene. In one's home county, the people know you and you know them. It is a face-to-face encounter, without electronics. There are no PR men to create images for mass consumption. An aspiring politician has to identify himself with the hopes, desires, and ideas of his constituents. If he fails to live up to his promises, the people can vote him out at the next election. Tough political experience has taught me that government at the local level can more truly reflect the will of the people than a faceless bureaucracy, thousands of miles removed from the scene. Our republic was created in such a way that people could control their own institutions.

When I was out campaigning, friends often came up and said, "George C., you made a good dogcatcher. You should make a good legislator." Or "We're going to make a dogcatcher a legislator." It had never occurred to me during my dog-catcher days that the job would help me win election to the legislature in 1946.

Following my victory in the primaries, I had to return to Montgomery to resume my legal duties in the attorney general's office.

We went to Mrs. Metcalf's boardinghouse, knowing she would

not turn us down. The old, three-story frame house with its white columns was downtown on Catoma Street. Mrs. Metcalf met us at the door with a friendly smile. "I know what you need and I have a spare room. Please keep the baby as quiet as you can. The railway men sleep during the day and I try not to disturb them."

I told her, "We will do our best to keep Bobbie Jo quiet."

Lurleen grinned and said, "What you mean is that I'll keep the baby quiet," in obvious reference to the fact that I would be away most of the day.

It was a splendid arrangement. The baby ate at the table and we never lacked for a baby sitter. Bobbie Jo played with the railway men and became the house favorite. Years later, when I ran for governor for the first time, I heard about the hand-painted signs on boxcars and engines supporting my candidacy. Above all else, I liked one sign they had on some boxcars: VOTE FOR WALLACE–HE'S ONE OF US.

We spent Christmas 1946 in Tuscaloosa with my wife's family.

One of my objectives, on being elected to the legislature, was to co-operate with the newly elected governor, Jim Folsom, in carrying out his program for the state of Alabama. A bloc had formed against him in the legislature to oppose all his programs. Many vindictive members could not swallow the fact that he had defeated the professionals, and they were embittered by his success. I did not join this bloc, because I felt the governor was entitled to a fair chance. We often did not agree, but he had been elected by a majority of the people and I intended to help him when I could.

During my first session in the legislature, I introduced an ambitious bill to build five new trade schools in rural Alabama. With only one trade school in the entire state, the need for more was desperate. I had often talked about a balanced economy and the need for Alabama to attract new industry. No industrial incentives would work, however, unless we had a trained labor pool in the state. Many of our young people had left the farms completely lacking in skills to enable them to compete in the large cities. It pained me to see them migrate from their home state, and I hoped that my trade-school bill would offer a remedy for this social problem.

It took hard work during the entire session to get my bill

passed. It was approved by the Senate on the final night of the legislative session. This remains one of my proudest accomplishments as a freshman legislator.

After the bill passed, Governor Folsom arranged with the state board of education to have the first school built in my Congressional district. It was named after my father, George C. Wallace. Dad had dreamed that someday Alabama would have these fine trade schools all over the state. His wish came true. Today we have twenty-nine trade schools serving all the people of Alabama.

In exchange for his support, Governor Folsom had extracted a promise from me to help him in the future, if he should need me. This promise put me into somewhat of a quandary later on, and I went to ex-Governor Sparkman for advice. He made short shrift of my indecision. "You made a promise, George. Keep it!" I fulfilled my promise by working along with two others to help re-elect Governor Folsom in 1954 (as his campaign manager for South Alabama).

I had first met Big Jim when he was campaigning in Barbour County for governor. He was incredibly tall—six foot eight—handsome, and very outgoing. The political pundits had predicted that his folksy and unorthodox ways would defeat him.

I remember him standing in front of the courthouse talking to the huge crowd that had gathered. He was an imposing figure, and he yelled in a booming voice, "They are making fun of me for using good old hillbilly music in my campaign. You see that Confederate statue over there? Well, men like that marched off to war with Lee and Jackson to the tune of country music. If country music was good enough for them, it's good enough for Big Jim." The crowd roared and stomped in approval.

Folsom approached me and held out his hand. "What's your name, son?"

"Wallace, sir."

He kept waving to the crowd. "Are you kin to Ed Wallace, who drowned in 1936?"

"Yes, that was my uncle."

He stopped waving and turned to me. "I worked with him in Washington, D.C., with the WPA. Good to see you." He walked back into the crowd. I had met Big Jim Folsom.

Folsom was a modern-day populist, and his style of campaigning broke all the rules of the professional politician. He drew large crowds on the stump and used country and Western bands for his easy style of speaking. The band was called the Strawberry Pickers.

He was elected governor in 1946, defeating Lieutenant Governor Handy Ellis in the general election. He ran again in 1954 and was elected for a second term by a larger popular vote than in his first election. I didn't support Big Jim in 1946, but I did in 1954, serving on his three-man campaign committee. Big Jim used to say, "This committee's job is to take politics out of politics." Exactly what he meant by this has always puzzled me.

I wrote his campaign kick-off speech in 1954, and that led my future opponents to insist that I had written all his speeches. The fact is that Governor Folsom didn't like to campaign with prepared speeches. He preferred to make a few notes and then deliver his speeches "off the cuff."

This opening speech called for more road building, more schools, higher teachers' salaries, and more aid to the aged. He stressed the need to reapportion the Legislature and update the state constitution.

My break with Governor Folsom came shortly after he was inaugurated. I felt that I was not allowed to play a strong enough role in guiding and directing the legislative program. Some of his cabinet members opposed me, and I had no alternative but to leave his camp. Many of these members were men that Big Jim had told me would not be appointed to the cabinet, and I knew I would be compromised politically if I remained. He made it clear that he did not need me—or want me around. In spite of this, when I ran for governor for the first time, in 1958, my political enemies called me a Folsom man. A study of the record will prove otherwise.

I could write many stories about Big Jim, but I'll leave that job to my wife, who is his niece. Alabamians can be grateful for what Big Jim started when he was their governor.

When the legislative session adjourned, Lurleen and I returned to Clayton. I began my first law practice in a one-room office above the local drugstore, paying a modest $7.50 a month rent.

In a small farming community you handle all kinds of cases: equity, divorce, criminal, and property damage. The criminal cases ranged from moonshining to one of murder. My first case involved a man accused of illegal distilling, a fairly frequent offense in the 1940s.

I knew this man was honest and highly respected in his community. It was hard to accept that he had gotten involved in anything illegal. I told him to sit down and tell me the whole story.

He had met a fast-talking ex-convict who had persuaded him that there was fast money to be made with a "still." Unfortunately, the ex-convict had been picked up and had implicated his hapless partner.

I asked my client point-blank, "Are you guilty of this offense?"

"Yes, I am," he answered forthrightly.

"Well, we cannot enter a not-guilty plea. What do you want me to do?"

"I want you to represent me before the parole board. Try to get me out on probation as soon as you can."

Judge Williams of Clayton was an old-fashioned man who believed the best way to prevent crime was to impose the maximum sentence on first offenders. He was a fine gentleman, scrupulously fair, but inflexible in his approach to crime and punishment. The jury probably would not have convicted my client, knowing that the judge never gave parole to first offenders. But with a guilty plea entered, the sentence was one year in the state prison. I went before the parole board immediately and explained the background of the case. They took my plea under study, and my client was released on probation after serving only about one week.

This same judge once sentenced a group of farmers for cattle stealing. One of the thieves was in his nineties, but the judge—who was nearly eighty himself—made no allowance for the man's age. Prison officials were astounded when the poor man arrived at the prison gates. He could hardly walk. Without waiting for legal authority, they put the old man in a car and sent him home. They later arranged for him to be legally pardoned.

I have always liked this story, because I feel the law must have a heart, and the officials acted in this case as human beings.

Judge Williams retired the year I ran for circuit-court judge. He lived to be nearly ninety-six, and he supported me for governor in 1958. He was a hard taskmaster for a young attorney practicing in his court, but his virtues far outweighed his faults. His grandfather had been the first Democrat elected to Congress after the War between the States, over a "Republican scalawag."

I soon found that criminal practice was excellent experience but would never make me rich. I handled criminal cases because I couldn't turn down someone who needed legal help.

I had run for the assignment as alternate delegate to the Democratic Convention in Philadelphia in 1948. Although I had won, I was not sure I could attend, because of my shortage of money. But some friends in Eufaula and Clayton got together and raised three hundred dollars to pay for my trip. I was doubly grateful when I found that most of the contributions had been in small amounts—two, three and five dollars.

My traveling schedule called for me to be in Montgomery, from where I was to drive to Philadelphia with a friend, Jimmy Faulkner, sharing expenses. Time was short, and my Eufaula friends arranged with a pilot, Peter Lunceford, to fly me to Montgomery—unaware of my fear of flying.

Lunceford was a fine pilot, and we arrived in Montgomery in time for me to leave with Jimmy Faulkner. This trip completely erased my hang-up about flying, and I have never since hesitated about taking air trips.

The environment in Philadelphia was highly charged. Harry Truman had come out with his celebrated civil rights program, which Southerners opposed on constitutional grounds. We felt the program infringed upon the rights of the states under the tenth Amendment. It's easy to charge "racial prejudice," but my personal opposition was based on strong fears that unconstitutional methods employed for so-called good ends could later be employed for bad ends. On issues where emotions are involved, I feel it is especially important for the Constitution to be an anchor, and not a sail subject to the winds of change. The states, in creating the federal government, granted only the most essential powers to the central government, retaining all nonspecified powers to themselves, the states. I cast my ballot for Richard Russell of Georgia and later supported Strom Thurmond, who ran on the Dixiecrat ticket.

Living with an ambitious young politician is no easy task for a wife. She must put up with his frequent absences from home and the excessive demands on his time and person. Lurleen and I had some minor squabbles over the money I had to spend on gasoline in order to campaign and attend political functions. We had inherited a 1938 Chevrolet from my grandfather when he died, and in this prewar car I traveled all over Barbour County running for the legislature.

Lurleen was easy to get along with, but when she felt that something was unfair she never hesitated to speak up. I recall the hassle caused by my Saturday afternoon poker games. She didn't mind the "afternoon" part of it, but she was irritated at the games that continued far into the night.

One hot Saturday afternoon, my cronies and I were playing under a large shade tree when Lurleen drove up in a borrowed car. Anger was etched into her face. She walked up to me, put Peggy Sue on my lap, and declared, "George, I can't wash and dry the clothes and take care of two children all at the same time." Without waiting for me to reply, she drove off.

Peggy Sue was definitely anti-poker. She fidgeted, screamed, and exposed my cards. In an attempt to prevent her from sabotaging the game, I gave an old man a dollar to show her the farm animals. She returned promptly and once more made a "friendly game" impossible.

Lurleen had proved her point. I picked up Peggy Sue and headed home. That was the end of my poker sessions.

No one really has any privacy in a small town, and stories about my poker playing had circulated freely. One day, a mother of one of my poker gang confronted me near my home. "George C., I'm ashamed of you," she said in outrage. "Here you are, a lawyer and Sunday school teacher, playing poker for money."

I cast my eyes down rather sheepishly, and she continued the inquisition. "I hope you have stopped, because if you have not, I am not going to vote for you again."

She couldn't have made a more effective threat. "I have quit playing poker," I reassured her, "and I don't have any intention of doing it again. Now, mind you, I don't promise I won't, because I just might." I added that I appreciated her vote and invited her to come visit us. I didn't mention the fact that her own son was one of the poker crowd. She continued to vote for me.

Apart from the hectic political pace, ours was typical of life in a small southern town. There were picnics with the children, movies, and church on Sunday. I taught a boys' Sunday school class, and when I saw them start to get restless I would abandon the lesson and start telling them war stories.

In 1952 I ran for judge of the Third Judicial District, which is made up of Barbour, Dale, and Bullock counties. I was elected by a three-to-one majority over a very distinguished and gentle opponent, Senator Preston Clayton, of Clayton and Eufaula. His grandfather had been a general in the Confederate Army, and the whole family had made important contributions to the state of Alabama. Senator Clayton remains a friend to this day, and I value his advice on political matters. He also served ably on the Alabama Supreme Court.

Senator Clayton had been a colonel in World War II, and during the heat of the campaign I jokingly remarked, "I want all of you colonels in the crowd to vote for my opponent, Preston Clayton, and I want all of you enlisted men to vote for me." An ex-colonel who had been on Corregidor during the war wrote to accuse me of trying to stir up class prejudice.

Lurleen and I bought our first home shortly after I began my service on the bench. We paid eighty-five-hundred dollars (with a bank loan, of course) for an old house belonging to our former landlady Mrs. Davis. It was a momentous event to have a home of our own after so many years of one-room, share-the-kitchen living, or two-room apartments in small homes. Thinking back to the days of the chicken house in Alamogordo, we were extremely happy.

I have a deep conviction about politics and courtrooms not mixing, and I tried at all times to keep both politics and race out of my court. I believe the record will show that I dispensed justice based on the law and the facts.

During the urban renewal program of the city of Eufaula, I tried a series of cases involving condemnation of property. These had been brought from a lower court on appeal by Fred Gray, a black attorney and later an important civil rights leader in Alabama. Gray's plea was that awards made in behalf of his clients, most of them black, had not been adequate. My court was flooded with appeals, and to expedite the judicial process, I tried more than one hundred cases in a single week. I arranged for one jury to go out and look at the properties involved at the same time another jury was being impaneled. We stipulated that arguments would be limited to three minutes for each side. In every instance, the largely white juries raised the amount of the awards for the black plaintiffs. This was a tribute to Fred Gray's ability as an attorney. He had earlier filed many motions involving constitutional issues and interpretations all the way to the Supreme Court.

After the last case had been heard and decided, Gray asked the court's permission to say a few words, and I still recall the substance of his remarks: "I wish to thank this court, the judge, the officers of the court, and the jury for their courtesy and consideration. I have never appeared in a more courteous and fairer court than this one, presided over by Judge Wallace." Not one of the cases was ever appealed.

One amusing incident sticks in my mind as an example of a witness confounding a judge. A trial involved several blacks charged with shooting each other. We were taking testimony from witnesses about what they had observed during the shooting. One old black witness testified that he had seen what had happened and proceeded to describe the events in detail. It turned out that he had been watching from a very considerable distance from the shooting, and I decided to pursue this question. "Tell me," I asked him, "just how far can you see?" He looked up at me and replied in all innocence, "Judge, how far is the sun?"

I stopped questioning him.

Another case, in which I had to be both judge and jury, involved a white friend and a black plaintiff. The state of Alabama required all companies employing a certain number of people to have workmen's compensation or their own insurance coverage. This small sawmill operator had neither, on the hope that there would never be an accident.

A young black man of eighteen or nineteen had lost his life in a work-related accident in my friend's sawmill. The young widow brought suit against the owner, asking for several thousand dollars' compensation. The facts were incontrovertible, and I ruled against my friend in favor of the widow. The verdict was upheld by the State Supreme Court on appeal.

The mill owner had to pay the damages out of his pocket. He was understandably unhappy about my decision and it took some time for the breach in our friendship to mend. He later supported me for governor and told everyone that if he ever had a case again, he would like Judge Wallace to hear it.

The full spectrum of cases came before me: civil suits, equity, criminal cases. But the most difficult for me were always the divorce suits. In spite of my efforts to bring the splitting couples back together, there was usually no alternative but to grant divorces. This pained me, especially when there were children involved. To watch mother and father cut each other to pieces in court and then each demand sole custody of a child disturbed me greatly.

My experience in divorce proceedings confirmed my conviction that the break-up of the family is a tragic social cancer. I remember reading in Gibbon's *Decline and Fall of the Roman Empire* that the increase in divorces coincided with Rome's period of decadence.

In 1900 there was one divorce for each hundred marriages. We are now approaching a one-to-two ratio. I think the results are evident in our society, and I pray that America can someday return to a more stable and responsible family life.

Probation poses another problem for a conscientious judge. I do not believe in probation for crimes of violence, even when it is a first offense. In other cases involving first offenders, I gave the matter careful study, trying to evaluate all the facts, and granted probation when I felt that the circumstances merited it. I had very few probation decisions go sour.

As a judge, I felt it was my duty not only to understand the law but to know and understand people, to see beneath the surface and try to evaluate the motivations of litigants. I soon learned that events and people are not always what they appear to be on the surface. A case in point comes to mind.

During the turbulence that swept our State in the mid-1960s, a man named Al Lingo, who headed the state police, was maligned by the mass media as a bigot and professional redneck racist. The art of character distortion has become a real force in our political life today, and what happened to Al Lingo is an example. Before becoming head of the state police he had been foreman of a jury that convicted a white man of killing a black man in Eufaula. All the witnesses against the defendant were black. The jury deliberated the case and brought in a verdict of guilty; the man was sentenced to life imprisonment.

Normally, a convicted murderer is not eligible for parole until he has served ten or twelve years of his sentence. But just a few years after the man's conviction, members of his family got up a petition to present to the parole board, requesting that the prisoner be paroled. Some members of the convicting jury signed the petition, but Al Lingo would not. Whatever his faults, I will remember Al Lingo as a man who tried to be scrupulously fair to all—black and white.

In 1956 I attended the Democratic Convention in Chicago as a delegate from Alabama and was chosen to represent my state on the platform committee. I was pleased that we were able to obtain a milder and more intelligent "civil rights" platform than the one in 1952. Extremists of both groups screamed about the platform, but the democratic system requires compromise and comity.

The convention nominated Adlai Stevenson as the Democratic candidate for the presidency. The old campaigner Harry Truman opposed the nomination, saying, "Stevenson can never win the election." His misgivings were very much like my feelings about Senator McGovern in the 1972 elections.

The vice-presidential nomination was fought out between Senator Estes Kefauver and Senator John Kennedy. I voted on the first ballot for Senator Gore, but later changed my vote to Senator Kennedy. Southern delegates opposed Kefauver because they felt he was too liberal and that Kennedy would be better for the interests of the South. Senator Kennedy in those days was far more conservative than he later was, and he received greater relative support from the South than from any other section. We became good friends, and when his book *Profiles in Courage* came out he sent me an autographed copy inscribed, "To my good friend, Judge George C. Wallace." I still treasure that book.

After an exciting and wearisome convention, I was glad to be back in Clayton to resume my duties as judge.

I'm not sure when I first decided I wanted to be governor of Alabama. Far back in grammar school, whenever my teachers asked about my ambitions, I would reply, "Someday I want to be governor." It surprised neither friends nor foes, therefore, when I announced my candidacy for governor in 1958.

One of the first things I had to learn in that first primary campaign was how to handle hecklers. Columbiana was the home town of one of the other candidates, Karl Harrison. As I was speaking at a rally in Columbiana, a school bus pulled up loaded with student supporters of the home-town favorite. They started to razz me and made it hard for me to be heard over the cheers and screams for Harrison.

"I know you have a fine candidate in the race," I told them, "but if you will just let me finish my speech, I'll get out of town." The promise to get out of town brought a cheer.

I looked directly at the students and said, "If you boys will be quiet, I'll see that you are promoted to the second grade." That didn't set well. Then I added, "I might even have the school closed down for you. How would you like that?"

The students' jeers turned into cheers.

These youngsters were amateurs, of course, compared to the hecklers I was to confront six years later at Harvard and other colleges. There I encountered in many instances real hate. The university students spat, screamed, and swung signs reading GOD IS LOVE.

By mid-March my campaign had caught fire. I proposed an educational program to put Alabama in the forefront of the South and give the state a public school system equal to that of any state in the Union. I pledged I would allocate part of my time as chief executive to traveling all over the United States seeking industries to locate in Alabama. I proposed increases in pensions for the elderly, a highway program to catch up with the rest of the nation, and an administration dedicated to honesty and integrity. As the campaign moved into April, I became the odds-on favorite to win the primary. Up to then, no one had recognized the closing speed of my opponent, Attorney General John Patterson.

John Patterson had made mighty few mistakes as attorney general. Many Alabamians were still suffering from a guilt complex about Phenix City, where crime, corruption, and vice had been a way of life for a generation. John's father, as attorney general, had decided to clean up the Phenix City mess. He was assassinated, and John replaced him as attorney general.

Subsequently, John Patterson cleaned up Phenix City, and his father's slayer was imprisoned. I have always admired John, and we are good personal friends today.

When the votes were counted in the first primary, Patterson had beaten me 196,859 to 152,435. A distant third was Jimmy Faulkner with 91,859.

I told my supporters, "I was trying for a run-off and I've made it. I hope none of you are disappointed about coming in second. We have come a long way, and we still have a good chance to win in the second primary and take the nomination." As a matter of fact, our chances were pretty bleak, but I intended to do my best.

It was a strange sort of campaign. I sometimes felt like a boxer dancing around the ring with no opponent. John Patterson appeared on the Hollywood TV show "This Is Your Life," but otherwise his campaign manager took no chances that in the last minute his candidate would commit a costly error. Patterson was sealed off from the press, television, and radio. The state was covered with billboards displaying his handsome face and carrying the line "Nobody's for Patterson but the people."

I was running behind, and there was little I could do about it. There was a strong and genuine sympathy vote for him.

As the general election date drew near, I did make some progress in closing the gap. I picked up some newspaper support, the most important being the Birmingham *News*, the largest paper in Alabama. I intensified my personal speaking engagements. This meant being on the road most of the time. Fortunately, I enjoyed a rigorous campaign then as I still do now. In my opinion, the campaign is one of the most exhilarating parts of political life.

A good friend, Billy Watson, was my traveling companion on those state-wide sweeps. Much older than I, Billy had a fine sense of humor and was the best antidote to fatigue and pressure.

He accompanied me when I spoke to civic groups and political rallies. Sometimes, when my morale dipped, I would ask, "Billy, how did you like my speech?" And in his dry way he would answer, "George, that speech was so good I nearly didn't go to sleep."

1. A little before my time, but this was Clio, Alabama, about 1900. (copy by Palmer Studio, Mobile)

2. First grade.

3. "Sunday" photo with a friend, Hilda Knight.

4. The Barbour Bantam at fifteen years of age.

5. Page in the Alabama state legislature; probably the key to my later interest in politics.

6. The University of Alabama boxing team, 1940. Even then I was on the right.

7. Glen Curlee and I as college students, probably up to some mischief.

8. Selling magazines door to door during the Depression was no easy task but we looked eager. I'm the serious one with the white pants.

9. The wartime Wallace family. Chronic housing shortages around military bases forced us to rent a converted chicken house in New Mexico.

. Everyone had a photo taken in the
ew uniform for the folks.

11. The crew of the *Sentimental Journey*. Left to right (top): Captain Robert Ray, pilot; Lieutenant Emil Kott, radar operator; Lieutenant Robert Lamb, navigator; Lieutenant George Harbinson, bombardier; Lieutenant Jason Riley, copilot; (front): Sergeant Art Feiner, gunner; Sergeant Richard Zind, radio operator; Sergeant George C. Wallace, flight engineer; Sergeant Johnny Petroff, gunner; Sergeant George Leahy, gunner; Sergeant Robert Bushhouse, central fire-control gunner.

12. A studio shot with Lieutenant Bob Lamb, navigator on the *Sentimental Journey*, taken after our return to the States in 1945.

I once asked him, "Did you enjoy the trip?" And he replied, "It was a wonderful trip. Don't take me on another one."

Patterson won the election for governor by a healthy margin of sixty-five thousand votes. Whoever the writer was who coined the phrase "Nobody's for Patterson but the people" knew what he was saying.

Back in my circuit court, a legal drama began unfolding on October 29, 1958. Crews Johnston, a Clayton attorney and former Barbour County prosecutor, filed a petition asking seizure of the Barbour County voting records. The petition charged electoral fraud in that unqualified voters were reported to have registered in Barbour County through misrepresentation to the board of registrars.

On November 21, Bullock County tax collector J. T. Ogletree filed a similar seizure request, charging that unqualified persons had registered.

On the basis of these petitions, I immediately ordered the voting records impounded for grand jury action.

In the meantime, delegates of the Civil Rights Commission had come to Alabama and wanted me to bring all the voter records to Montgomery for them to examine. This was contrary to state law, which prohibits voting records from being removed from the county. Furthermore, I was holding them for grand jury investigation, which I felt took precedence over any civil rights investigation. I issued a statement to that effect: "I cannot see how the Civil Rights Commission, which is a part of the executive branch of the government, can even ask for records lawfully impounded by the circuit court of Barbour and Bullock counties."

We told the Civil Rights Commission that the records they wanted had been impounded by the grand jury and could not be removed from the county; we said they could see the records when the grand jury was through with them.

Federal Judge Frank M. Johnson then issued an order for me to appear before the Civil Rights Commission—which, in my judgment, was illegal. You don't summon a judge; you appeal cases. I had impounded the records, and if I had done so improperly then they should have filed a proper motion in the court. But they did not.

I made my position clear: "This action is contrary to our form of government and separation of powers. I will jail any civil rights agent who attempts to get the records."

When I failed to appear before the commission on December 8, Judge Johnson then issued an order for me to take the records to Montgomery. Once more I ignored the order. Governor-elect John Patterson, who was still serving as attorney general; former Governor Chancey Sparks; Mr. Preston Clayton, who had been my opponent for circuit judge; Archie Grubb; Sam LeMaistre, and all the other members of the Barbour County Bar Association who had voluntarily joined to defend me, went before the court and obtained a hearing for January 5, 1959.

I was anxious to give full publicity to the threat of federal power, and I didn't want the people to be confused by the legal complexities of the charges and countercharges. I issued a statement that read:

"Roman holiday investigations, held in a Federal courtroom, surrounded by a circus atmosphere with television cameras and hired publicity agents, have stemmed from just three complaints in Barbour County and one in Bullock County. All this expenditure of the taxpayers' money, insofar as these two counties are concerned, was made on the pretext of protection of civil rights of four disgruntled individuals and at the expense of the rights of a duly elected judge and other state officials. The manner in which this investigation has been conducted smacks of publicity and propaganda and has shown a total disregard for the courts of this State and its officials. The efforts on my part have been to protect the dignity of the State's courts and the rights of the people of this State."

I concluded with: "The time has come when we must stand up and defend the rights of the people of Alabama, regardless of personal sacrifices." Thus was born the campaign slogan "Stand Up for Alabama."

Before the Civil Rights Commission could bring me into court, I assembled my grand juries, first in Barbour County and then in Bullock. I made the same statement to both grand juries: "When I turn these records over to you, I realize I no longer have control over them. The grand jury is the supreme investigative body of this county. I am willing to accept whatever consequences there may be for my action in impounding the voting records and in turning them over to you."

I was also motivated by the fact that I was ending my term as circuit court judge and did not want to leave the problem with my brother, Jack Wallace, who had been elected to succeed me as judge.

On the morning of January 15, while I remained in my hotel room awaiting developments, my attorneys walked into Judge Johnson's court. I took this position with respect to the order of the court and the Civil Rights Commission for one reason: I wanted to test the validity of a federal court order to a state official. I believed this was unconstitutional and should be tested by the highest court in the land, the Supreme Court.

I do not believe in disobedience of court orders and would have obeyed a final order on this matter because unless we have obedience to orders—whether we like them or not—the seeds of anarchy are sown. And for a nation to survive we must have stability and order.

Judge Johnson dismissed the civil action involving the Civil Rights Commission's investigation of the voting records of Barbour and Bullock counties. He then ordered criminal contempt proceedings to be instituted against me and instructed me to appear in court on January 26 to show cause, if any, why I should not be punished for contempt.

At the stroke of ten on the morning of January 26, 1959, Judge Johnson strode into the courtroom with a grim and determined expression. I submitted a written statement in which I admitted I had defied the federal court's order directing me to allow the Civil Rights Commission's agents to inspect the voting records. I stated I was not guilty of contempt inasmuch as I was acting in my capacity as circuit court judge. Giving the records to the grand juries was an act of a judicial nature, and as a judge I had no other alternative. I feel that the order was an illegal order and would be set aside upon appeal if the ruling was against me. However, I would have obeyed a final order in the matter.

I did not present any witnesses, nor did I ask my attorneys to cross-examine any of the government's witnesses. The jury foremen from Barbour and Bullock counties testified that I had turned over the records to the grand juries without issuing instructions to make them available to the Civil Rights Commission. The grand juries had allowed agents for the commission to see the records, but only under strict vigilance.

After my testimony, Judge Johnson recessed the court until 2 P.M. that day. On reconvening, he delivered a most amazing opinion, finding, in effect, that I had actually *co-operated* with the Civil Rights Commission agents. I was acquitted of the contempt charge. In summing up, Judge Johnson said:

> This court further finds that, even though it was accomplished through a means of subterfuge, George C. Wallace did comply with the order of this court concerning the production of the records in question. As to why the devious methods were used, this court will not now judicially determine. In this connection, the court feels it sufficient to observe that if these devious means were in good faith considered by Wallace to be essential to the proper exercise of his state judicial functions, then this court will not and should not comment upon these methods. However, if these devious means were for political purposes, then this court refuses to allow its authority and dignity to be bent or swayed by such politically generated whirlwinds.
>
> The defendant, George C. Wallace, is ordered to be and is hereby found not guilty of contempt of this court and stands discharged.

I made no effort to conceal my frustration over this ridiculous turn of events, and I immediately issued a statement, as the statements of the events written in the order were in no manner born out by any evidence:

> The action today only goes to show if you will back them to the wall they'll hunt any way to back down. . . . I pleaded guilty to failing to deliver the voter registration records to agents of the Civil Rights Commission. All the testimony that can be inspected when the transcript is published will disclose that no witness testified otherwise. Since there was a grave constitutional question involved, I had hoped to take it to a higher authority, but now that I have been acquitted, I believe this justifies my militant stand against the efforts of the Civil Rights Commission to take over the courts of Alabama. . . . It was my position and is still my position that we have here a case of federal authority, and I was willing to risk my freedom in order to test the question at this time, as I felt an opinion should be rendered on this important question. The whole matter arose as a result of my doing my duty as circuit judge. I did my duty and pleaded guilty to

the failure to bow to the wishes of the court, and if the judge holds this is not a contempt, then I have no control over such conclusion.

I respect the dignity and integrity of this court, as this is a government of laws and not of men; however, I felt very strongly that if I passively submitted to the orders of the federal court in this instance, under the conditions as they were, our state courts would have been plowed under by judicial edict.

As to the "devious methods employed" referred to by the court in its decision, I turned the voter records over to the grand jury to do with as they saw fit—all testimony of the hearing verifies this. To call this "devious" shows a lack of understanding of the independence and procedure of our state courts. As to the alleged statement of "whirlwind politics," there is no testimony before the court on this subject either directly or indirectly.

These characters from the evil Civil Rights Commission and Justice Department were backed to the wall—they were defied and backed down. It has been apparent they were hunting a way out.

Since that time, we have seen the power of federal judges grow to the point where no aspect of our lives is immune. In Alabama, a federal judge tells us how to run our schools, how the state must tax its property owners, how a schoolboy may wear his hair, how the geographical boundaries of our political districts must be set, and even how we will run our mental institutions.

This was the first skirmish. Forces were gathering for more assaults on state institutions, and I was preparing to battle with the giant, the federal judiciary.

While in law school, I had memorized the words of Thomas Jefferson, and they have stuck with me ever since:

> It has long, however, been my opinion, and I have never shrunk from its expression (although I do not choose to put it into a newspaper nor, like a Priam in armour, offer myself its champion), that the germ of dissolution of our Federal government is in the constitution of the Federal judiciary as an irresponsible body (for impeachment is scarcely a scarecrow) working like gravity by night and by day, gnawing a little today and a little tomorrow, and advancing its noiseless step like a thief, over the

field of jurisdiction, until all shall be usurped from the States, and the government of all be consolidated into one. To this I am opposed: because when all government, domestic and foreign, in little as in great things shall be drawn to Washington as the center of all power, it will render powerless the checks provided of one government on another, and will become as venal and oppressive as the government from which we separated.

FIERCE CONTACT WITH LIFE

The Tenth Amendment to the Constitution: "The powers not delegated to the United States by the Constitution, nor prohibited by it to the States, are reserved to the States respectively."

Lincoln said: "We the people are rightful masters of both Congress & the courts, not to overthrow the Constitution, but to overthrow the men who pervert it."

The strain of my hard-fought gubernatorial campaign and my clash with the federal courts had left me worn and haggard. I needed a few weeks of rest to recuperate.

The unsuccessful bid for the governorship had made me new friends and supporters all over Alabama. I knew I had a firm base from which to launch a second campaign, in 1962. The next election was still four years away, but I started preparing for it immediately after my defeat.

To support my family, I practiced law in Clayton and kept a second office in Montgomery with my brother Gerald. If I had been content to devote my full time to a law practice, I could have made a good living at it. But I had set my heart on being governor. All else, my legal practice and making money, were secondary.

Lurleen justifiably protested that I was away from home even more than before. I traveled the state almost continuously, keeping before the people my ideas about state and national government. I talked mostly about the state's need for more funds for education, more industries, more roads, more help to the elderly, more hospitals, and the necessity of eliminating the liquor grafters. Materially, Alabama needed more of everything.

A good friend once asked me what motivated me. I couldn't

give a simple answer. Human motives are complex. I did tell him I wanted to see our country return to the principles on which it was founded. I wanted the political leaders to think more about states' rights and local government and to halt the destruction of individual liberty and personal responsibility.

I felt strongly that we could no longer hide our head in the sand while the ideology of our forefathers was being attacked. We were faced then and today with the notion that if central government assumes enough authority, enough power over people, it can provide a utopian life—that if allowed to dictate, to forbid, to require, to distribute, to issue edicts, and to judge what is best for all, it will produce only good. It will then be our father—and our God.

St. Paul, in his letter to the Corinthians, wrote: "For if a trumpet give an uncertain sound, who shall prepare for battle?" I did not intend to make an uncertain sound.

After the joy of two daughters and a fine son, George, Jr., and shortly before the start of my second gubernatorial race, Lurleen and I were made extremely happy by the birth of our fourth child. We named this bundle of joy Janie Lee Wallace, after my favorite hero, Robert E. Lee of Virginia.

Our joy was clouded when the doctors discovered some suspicious-looking tissue during Lurleen's Caesarean delivery. I feared that the pathologist's report would show cancer. To make sure no mistake was made, we sent the suspect tissue to different laboratories to be examined.

The reports all came back negative, although two were cautiously so. One pathologist thought the tissue could be malignant, but he could not be sure.

Later, to remove all doubt from our minds, we had Lurleen examined by Dr. Scarborough of Emory University. This very fine doctor, who was later to die from cancer himself, checked Lurleen thoroughly and gave her a clean bill of health. Lurleen had less than seven years to live, but mercifully we did not know it then.

Before the start of the 1962 campaign, Lurleen decided that she had no intention of being a "campaign widow." She announced that she would hit the campaign trail with me.

We rented an apartment in Montgomery so we could be centrally located during the campaign. Lurleen's mother stayed with the children while we traveled through sixty-seven counties. Every few days, Lurleen would dash back to see how the children were doing, then return to campaign with me.

Lurleen enjoyed traveling and meeting people all over the state. She learned firsthand how the people felt and thought about issues. I remember her telling me, "Alabamians are the finest and the warmest-hearted people in the world."

She loved the people and they loved her. They sensed her warmth and sincerity.

Following my 1958 defeat, Bill Jones had told me, "George C., I have seen you walk a mile to shake hands with a farmer in his field. You made speeches to small groups when you could have had large crowds if we had organized our campaign better. The next campaign is going to be handled differently." Everything he said was true, and we did run our campaign more efficiently in 1962.

I won the May 1 primary against strong opposition, polling 207,062 to the runner-up deGraffenreid's 160,704 votes. Jim Folsom polled 159,640 votes but was eliminated in the run-off election in June.

Folsom switched his support to deGraffenreid, making the outcome in the run-off election more uncertain for me. When a reporter asked me about Jim Folsom's decision, I answered simply, "Folsom is entitled to vote for anyone he wishes to, just like any other private citizen."

DeGraffenreid conducted a spirited campaign, and I never at any moment felt sure of victory. He was tall, handsome, and a fine speaker. He drew large crowds and was a very worthy adversary.

I kept hammering away at the same issues: quality education for all, local control of government, more industrial development, honesty and economy in state government, aid to the elderly, and a strong pledge to continue the fight to preserve the U. S. Constitution.

Many of my local stands were later to become national postures.

In one small town I declared: "The Supreme Court has made it against the law to read the Bible in public schools. Certain northern newspapers and magazines, in an effort to be derogatory against Alabama, said, 'Alabama is in the Bible Belt.' What is so wrong about being for the Bible?"

Shortly before the run-off election, Jim Folsom released to the press a personal attack on me. It failed, because I believe most voters want to consider the issues and do not like character assassination. To me, that kind of thing degrades the political process and all involved in it.

The run-off election was a smashing victory. I had won by a margin of more than seventy thousand votes.

The inauguration was seven and a half months away. There was considerable work to do and I used the time to prepare for my first administration.

My long-nursed ambition was finally realized when I was sworn in as governor of the sovereign state of Alabama on January 14, 1963. The day was unusually cold and wet, disappointing my family's hopes for good weather for the crowds that had come to Montgomery. I personally prepared for the cold by wearing two union suits under my formal attire. The press appropriately referred to my underwear as "confederate suits." Despite the biting cold, nothing could dampen our spirits.

Lurleen was radiant as we made our way to the inauguration stand that had been erected on the steps of the capitol building. She whispered in my ear, "I'm so glad you never gave up. I'm so proud, and whatever sacrifices I made it was worth it."

My brother Judge Jack Wallace administered the oath of office. Seated in the stands were outgoing Governor John Patterson and ex-Governors James E. Folsom and Frank Dixon. Former Governor Ross Barnett and Lieutenant Governor Paul Johnson of Mississippi were among the distinguished guests from other states. And with us on this happy day, naturally, were all of my family and my wife's family.

Mom Sanders had come from Arkadelphia as our honored guest. I assigned a state trooper to escort her to all the social functions of the day.

After recognizing the outgoing governor and the other dignitaries, I began my formal address. I repeated the pledges I had made during the campaign, adding a strong plea for a return to the "strong, simple faith and sane reasoning of our founding fathers." I referred to the hated national racism of Hitler's Germany, charging that Hitler's concepts were being revived under the guise of "liberalism." "As the national racism of Hitler's Germany subjected a national minority to the whim of a national majority, so the international racism of the liberals seeks to persecute the international white minority at the whim of the international colored majority."

I vigorously denied the Supreme Court view that our Constitution was outdated and must be changed. I spoke of men who had "yielded to the temptation to play God." "We do not defy," I insisted, "for there is nothing to defy, since as free men we do not recognize any government right to give freedom or to deny freedom." I quoted Thomas Jefferson: "The God who gave us life, gave us liberty at the same time; no king holds the right of liberty in his hands." "Nor," I added, "does any ruler in American government."

I pledged as governor to "stand up for Alabama" and asked the people to stand with me, "to give courageous leadership to millions of people throughout this nation who look to the South for their hope in this fight to win and preserve our freedoms and liberties."

The parade that followed my inauguration was magnificent. There were 170 bands, among them the University of Alabama's "Million-Dollar Band," directed by Colonel Carlton Butler. In spite of the cold, there were almost a hundred floats and twenty-one marching units—and several of the poor majorettes had to be treated for frostbite.

It was a long-suffering crowd that endured the biting cold for more than three hours to watch the splendid parade. The day ended with a gala inauguration ball in the Garret Coliseum. That night we slept in the Governor's Mansion on Perry Street.

Alabama's Governor's Mansion was built more than seventy years ago. Its ante-bellum architecture is tastefully elegant. A huge staircase dominates the interior. Left of the staircase are a sitting room and dining room; to the right are a living room and a glass-enclosed sun porch. Off these main rooms are a den, a bath, and a small dining room. This latter room has always been preferred by my family.

After Lurleen became first lady, she opened the mansion to the public. She ran the mansion while I attended to state business. She was invariably up and about at 7 A.M. and generally remained on the go until late at night. She would often say to me, "If I had a whole day free, I don't think I'd know what to do with it."

Lurleen supervised preparation of the meals but left the cooking to the kitchen staff. Sometimes we had so many guests that it took all hands to get the job done, and Lurleen often pitched in and helped.

My pledge to have a "dry" administration was easy to keep. Lurleen and I were both teetotalers.

It did not take us long to be suspicious and cautious of the fawning and overfriendly newsmen. A reporter from *Newsweek* persuaded Lurleen that he was going to write a pro-Wallace article (so rare a thing in the '60s that we should have immediately become suspicious). He wanted to be with us constantly, and Lurleen went out of her way to be nice to the fellow.

One of the pro-Wallace comments *Newsweek* published was: "The Governor makes sucking sounds when he eats." In time you grow callous about this sort of journalism and pay little attention to it.

Lurleen usually had a simple answer for the personal attacks on me: "I have been married to my husband for twenty-five years. I know what kind of man he is." Whether or not I was ever a hero to Lurleen, I am grateful for her staunch loyalty.

Not long after my inauguration as governor, proceedings were begun to enroll two Negroes in the University of Alabama. The stage was set for the "stand in the schoolhouse door."

The issue did not involve the color of the students, as the board of trustees of the university was already moving in the direction of non-discrimination. For me, the issue was whether local and state institutions could survive when the "force cult" of big government was rapidly destroying them by federal court orders enforced by the threat of contempt action or, even more intimidating, the use of the Army in event of non-compliance.

I had told the people of Alabama during the 1962 campaign that, if elected, I would refuse to abide by any illegal federal court order. I intended to stand firm and meet the storm head on.

While the question of the admission of the two students was being processed through the court, the politicians were busy. Attorney General Robert Kennedy arrived to see me on April 26. My staff and I welcomed the Attorney General to Alabama and did our best to make his visit a safe one. I instructed my security director, Al Lingo, to place full protective forces around the capitol and to make certain no one was admitted to the governor's office without a security check.

I explained to the Attorney General that in order to avoid any misunderstanding about our conversation, I was going to make a tape recording of everything we said. A copy would be given to the Attorney General, and the tapes would not be released without the consent of both of us. Our conversation began, witnessed by members of my staff and the Attorney General's staff.

Robert Kennedy was businesslike, and at the first opportunity brought up the matter of the students entering the University of Alabama. He wanted assurances that I would not block their entry and that the whole thing could be achieved with civilian authority. I merely reaffirmed my original stand. I believe nothing was gained by this conversation.

On May 13, I flew to Muscle Shoals to meet President Kennedy, who had come to Alabama to celebrate the thirtieth anniversary of the Tennessee Valley Authority. I had known President Kennedy since 1956, when I met him at the Democratic Convention, and I had supported his nomination for Vice-President. We differed politically, but I had always liked him because of his agreeable personality. I recall, when we left the helicopter, his hair had been messed up and we went into the men's room to groom ourselves for the public appearance. He was an extremely good-looking man and wanted to look his best when he spoke. He received a warm reception, even though most of the people were opposed to his political views as they pertained to the state of Alabama.

Later, we flew to Huntsville, where the President was to speak at the Space Center. When we were getting into the helicopter, the President said, "Where would you like to sit?" I replied, "Mr. President, you can sit on the left and I'll sit on the right." He laughed, and it was the beginning of an enjoyable ride to Huntsville.

In his speech he omitted any reference to school integration but mentioned the demonstrations going on in Birmingham. He seemed anxious to have them end, as I was.

President Kennedy asked me, "Governor, can't we just work it out for a few blacks to be employed in the business firms in Birmingham?" I answered, "Mr. President, blacks have been employed for a long time in Birmingham. They may not have the high positions you and others might wish them to have, but that, in my judgment, is for the owner of the business to decide. I have no objection to the businessmen hiring who they want to. But I do object to the idea of having the government telling businessmen what they can and cannot do."

The demonstrations mentioned by President Kennedy had broken out in Birmingham as a prelude to the main act, the taking over of our schools by the judicial and executive branches of our government.

The demonstrations had been touched off by the bombing of a black church, in which four little children had died. This dastardly and insane bombing had been done by extremists—white or black—the kind of people who kill for political ends. I had no intention of turning the state over to *agents provocateurs* and mobs. I called on every available policeman and state trooper to bring law and order back to Birmingham.

With their help, and through the calm and forbearance of the black and white populations, the situation in Birmingham was brought under control. There was still tension, but the authorities had restored order, and we did not need any outside help to keep the peace.

President Kennedy, however, without legal or statutory grounds, dispatched three thousand U.S. troops to Alabama, while publicly admitting that no federal law was being violated in Birmingham. I insisted then and I insist now that it is not the function of the federal government to maintain law and order inside a state unless there is an armed insurrection against the United States.

I wired President Kennedy, asking by what authority he had sent federal troops to Alabama. I then filed suit, as governor, against the federal government for illegally sending U.S. troops under the guise of law. The Justice Department had dug down deep into history to resurrect the anti-rebellion U. S. Code, Title 10, Section 333, which permitted sending U.S. troops to the South after the Civil War in case of rebellion.

In my suit I asked the Supreme Court to declare unconstitutional the government's use of federal troops and to declare the Fourteenth Amendment unconstitutional by virtue of its illegal ratification. The court denied the motion.

On May 24, the Justice Department petitioned the U. S. District Court in Birmingham to prohibit me from interfering with the enrollment of the black students in the University of Alabama. The same court enjoined me—in an order issued by Judge Seybourn Lynn on June 5—from blocking or interfering with enrollment by black students.

Because of my covenant with the people of Alabama, to resist —within the law—the systematic destruction of the Constitution, I refused to comply with what I considered illegal federal court interference in affairs clearly belonging to the states. In addition, I was aware that if I failed to make a stand, the situation could lead to violence—something I did not want to happen.

In early June I appeared on the television show "Meet the Press," with Mr. Spivak and his press panel. As I expected, this news inquisition was out to demolish me and the people of the South. Fortunately, I kept my temper and presented my views politely. I was to have many more encounters with the news media.

Frank McGee asked me, "Governor Wallace, is it not possible that the constitutional questions you speak of could be raised without your physically standing in the schoolhouse door, and is it possible that you are hoping to have yourself arrested?"

I pointed out to Mr. McGee the necessity of awakening the country to the dangers of an all-powerful central government. "No, I am not hoping to have myself arrested at all, but I made a commitment in the campaign for governor that I would do this, and I feel this is a good and dramatic way to alert Americans to what is happening in their country."

Asked if I would go peacefully if arrested, I said I would—that I had no intention of fighting the federal government with force. I hammered at the non-violence theme, emphasizing that I had asked all people to stay away from the university campus unless they had specific authorization to be there.

The countdown had started. I ordered five hundred national guardsman to Tuscaloosa to patrol the campus at the University of Alabama. I intended to make sure no one would enter the campus to disrupt the proceedings on June 11. The President was notified that the Guard's presence was for the purpose of keeping the peace, and not to prevent the enrollment of the black students. President Kennedy, at a press conference, acknowledged that Governor Wallace was doing his best to keep law and order in his state.

I went on TV and asked the people of Alabama to stay away from the campus at Tuscaloosa. On Sunday, June 9, all the daily papers in Alabama gave prominent display to my plea for law and order.

On Saturday, June 8, Attorney General Robert Kennedy talked with my staff by telephone, trying to find out what I intended to do. He was told that I would do exactly what I had announced I would do.

Looking back on the event, I recall that I went to bed early Monday night, June 10, and rose early the next day. I wanted to be fully rested.

The attempts by the University of Alabama to make sure that all members of the press would enjoy equal treatment met with some journalistic absurdities. A restraining line had been painted in white to prevent any disruption of the proceedings. A few of the liberal reporters complained about the color of the paint.

The TV networks became involved in a violent disagreement over procedures until NBC and CBS agreed on a pool. But this agreement came only after we threatened to allow only movie cameras on the campus.

I left my hotel room at 9:30 A.M. John Kohn shook my hand and said, "You have divine blessing today, Governor. There is absolute peace here. It is a great tribute to the city and to the state—the people have shown great dignity. Good luck and may God bless you." His remarks moved me deeply.

I arrived at the university at nine-fifty, with the heat already at 95 degrees. At ten forty-eight the students arrived, accompanied by Nicholas Katzenbach, assistant attorney general, and his staff from the Justice Department.

I stood in the door and waited for the action to begin. Katzenbach came forward without the students and, obviously nervous, approached me. He identified himself and said he had a proclamation from the President of the United States. He held in his hand a "cease and desist" order for me not to interfere with the registration of the students. I was now in violation not only of a judicial decree but of a presidential order as well.

Katzenbach then said: "I have come here to ask you now for unequivocal assurance that you will permit these students, who, after all, merely want an education in the great university . . ."

I interrupted him bitingly, "Now, you make your statement, because we don't need your speech." He wiped his brow and restated the presidential order. I then read a five-minute prepared statement tracing the growth of the Constitution and stating my refusal "to willingly submit to illegal usurpation of power by the central government."

Katzenbach finally stuttered, "I take it from the statement that you are going to stand in the door and that you are not going to carry out the orders of the court and that you are going to resist us. Is that so?" I replied, "I stand on my statement." Those were my last words to Katzenbach.

Three more times he asked me to step aside and I refused. He then turned and went back to his waiting car. I had no doubt about what would happen next. I could resist civil authority, but not the power of the U. S. Army.

Moments later, the Alabama National Guard was federalized. Four hours later, a company of the troops was on the campus. Brigadier General Henry Graham and four enlisted men stood before me. Graham saluted me and said, "Sir, it is my sad duty to ask you to step aside under orders of the President of the United States."

I returned his salute and said, "I want to make a statement."

"Certainly, sir," Graham courteously replied. He stepped to one side smartly, and I spoke to him and his men:

"But for the unwarranted federalization of the Alabama National Guard, I would at this moment be your commander-in-chief. In fact, I am your commander-in-chief. As governor of this state, this is a bitter pill to swallow.

"If Alabama citizens will continue to be calm and restrained, it will help us win. We must not have violence today, or any other day.

"The National Guard is made up of men who live within our borders. They are our brothers.

"Alabama is winning this fight against federal interference because we are awakening the people to the trend toward military dictatorship in this country.

"I am returning to Montgomery to continuing working for constitutional government to benefit all Alabamians—black and white."

I stepped aside and left, motivated only by my desire to avoid violence.

I realized that the fight had to be continued on other grounds and in another arena. The national press, radio, and television had consistently maligned and distorted the attitude of the South by projecting a false and stereotyped image. It seemed incredible to me that our country in such a short space of time had forgotten what the South had given to this great land: George Washington, the father of his country; Thomas Jefferson, the author of the Declaration of Independence; and Patrick Henry, the firebrand patriot. Alabama, the "Heart of Dixie," which in wartime had produced more Medal of Honor winners than any other state on a per capita basis, was to receive more than its fair share of the media's contempt. Why so vigorous an attack on a region and its institutions? Perhaps I can answer the question in part.

The leftist liberal must first destroy regional and national patriotism before he can inject his slave-state philosophy with any hope of success. Fragment, alienate, and corrupt. Then the ground is fertile for the takeover. This determined revolution can be stopped only by a strong counterforce of faith in American institutions and traditions.

To make my views known in other parts of the country, I embarked on a speaking tour of U.S. colleges and universities. I decided to begin my speaking foray that fall in what was then referred to as "enemy territory": the Ivy League schools.

Prior to going to New England for my first speech, I had sent my very able press secretary, Bill Jones, to Boston to make all the arrangements. One morning, while he and his staff were breakfasting in the hotel dining room, a friendly waitress was intrigued by their deep South accent. "You fellows sure have an accent. Where are you from?" Bill Tyus, one of the pilots who had flown my aides North, looked up from his breakfast and replied dryly, "No, ma'am, you have the accent."

My first speech was at Harvard University. I had been told to expect rudeness in the form of hissing by the students, and not to be disappointed if I got no applause at the end of my remarks. To the discomfort of the liberals, I was applauded frequently by the students; and whether or not my speech on the Constitution made any converts I cannot say. I received a thunderous ovation when I finished.

As I prepared to leave the auditorium, my security staff told me there was a large "non-violent" group outside in an ugly mood, and that it would be necessary to leave by an underground passage. It was then I became acquainted with every steampipe in old Sanders Hall. While we were led through a maze of pipes, the beatniks screamed and sang the now familiar "We Shall Overcome" outside the auditorium.

Glen Curlee told me that my friend Billy Watson had gone outside for a breath of air and had been caught up in the marching and demonstrating by the protesters. Billy was nearly seventy years of age and bore a striking resemblance to President Eisenhower.

For the rest of his life Billy would tell about marching with the protesters and singing "We Shall Overcome." He had decided that the only way to get out alive was to sing lustily and edge his way to the sidelines to escape.

I needed Glen Curlee and Billy Watson to provide the lighter moments during our strenuous tour.

During a question-and-answer period, one black student asked me, "Would you run on a ticket with a black man?" I couldn't help smiling, then winking at him: "Between you and me we might get rid of the crowd in Washington. We might just run on the same ticket."

I enjoyed speaking to the students. Most of them were eager to know what I thought about the political and social issues of the day. Many of them had been exposed to a smattering of theoretical socialism and communism but had no instruction in how a constitutional republic functions. More than a few had an academic exposure to Marx and Engels, mixed with the brainwashing confusion of the media's presentation of current social and political events. It was saddening to see how many students had never heard of, let alone read, Locke, Jefferson, or Montesquieu. Why hadn't they been taught something of our country's historical and political roots? No wonder the nation was in such straits, when in our best universities the students were without any knowledge of how and why the founders of our country had created a constitutional republic with the separation of powers into three branches of government. I hope the day will come when no university will issue a liberal-arts degree without requiring stiff courses in U.S. history and the Constitution.

Several times on my New England tour I had attacked the policies of President Kennedy. But I always made it clear that my differences were political and not personal. I returned to Alabama with the intention of going to the West Coast in three or four weeks—and then came the tragic news that our President was dead.

I had just dedicated a new high school in Haleyville. During the luncheon following the dedication, we were told the President had been slain. I declared thirty days of mourning in Alabama and flew to Washington to pay my respects to the Kennedy family.

Later, when I returned to Washington for the funeral services at Arlington Cemetery, we were met at the airport by a member of the national press. This callous news carrier asked, "Are you glad now you have a southern president?" I was disgusted with him and showed it, but I merely replied, "This transcends any political questions." I hurried away from the unfeeling clod.

Although I was John Kennedy's political opponent, I deplored his killing, and I felt the loss of a great and good heart from the American scene. Years later, when I was recovering from the Bremer bullets, members of the Kennedy family came to see me in the Holy Cross Hospital. This touched me greatly. Cornelia and I will never forget the kind offer of Ethel Kennedy to use her home while we were in Maryland.

President Kennedy's death brought a halt to my speechmaking for the rest of the year. We had a new President, but the issues had not changed. Under a smokescreen of emotionalism and misrepresentation, Congress was preparing a civil rights bill which, if passed, would affect the life of every American.

With the news media feeding tranquilizing pabulum to the people, I knew that someone had to alert Americans to what this pernicious piece of legislation proposed to do to them. I was convinced then, and remain convinced, that the real enemies of our country were those who sought more central authority to vanquish freedom in the name of freedom—those who wanted to destroy human rights in the name of civil rights—and those who inspired hatred and chaos in the name of love and peace.

I took off for my western tour in January 1964. My main purpose was to place the facts before the people, to tell them about the civil rights bill, and to meet with industrialists to encourage them to locate in Alabama. I was heartened by the large crowds that turned out to hear me.

My reception in Tucson was warm and friendly. When I told the local newsmen that the troops used to integrate the University of Alabama should have been used in Cuba, they cheered. Some newsmen have their own ideas and their own conscience.

I called the civil rights bill "the involuntary-servitude act of 1964," and I was applauded frequently. Outside, a line of pickets carried the usual signs.

I told a UCLA audience that I was not against non-discrimination, and that was exactly what the 1964 civil rights bill intended to do: discriminate. I said: "I support non-discrimination, but I am against the government of the United States, in the name of civil rights, trying to control the property rights of the people, of trying to control the seniority list of labor unions and labor-union apprenticeship. That is why I feel that the so-called civil rights bill is not in the interest of any citizen, regardless of race."

I continued by asking to have the civil rights bill put to a national referendum. I said the Johnson administration was afraid to trust it to a vote of the American people. The audience was courteous, but I don't think I converted many that day.

That same afternoon, I held a press conference in the Statler Hilton Hotel. A reporter from India began to attack the South and its customs. He did not ask questions, he made accusations. I stopped him promptly. "I suggest you go home to India and work to end the rigid caste system before you criticize my part of the United States. In India a higher caste will not even deign to shake hands with a lower caste. Yet you can't see the hypocrisy in your double standard." He made a hasty retreat.

This same India has received billions of dollars of U.S. taxpayers' money, technical aid, and food. Yet while they hold out both hands to get more largess, they insult us in the UN and, before the press of the world, call us "imperialist pigs." Just how much Indian leaders believe in democracy is evident in the dictatorial methods used to protect Mrs. Gandhi against prosecution for alleged political shenanigans.

It was at UCLA that I told the press, "You know, free speech can get you killed." My security advisers had warned me that I would have a difficult time and probably wouldn't be allowed to finish my speech. We entered the auditorium from the rear to avoid a confrontation with the "non-violent" protesters. These "free speech" advocates were there to make certain I didn't have an opportunity to exercise my right to free speech. Their failure to recognize their own incongruity has always puzzled me.

Up front, a leader of CORE was directing his crowd in rhythmic chants—"Wallace Must Go"—and then they all joined in singing "We Shall Overcome." It was sung beautifully.

My introduction by the vice-chancellor of UCLA was the usual: "I would like to present a man whose position is one with which most of you disagree, as I do myself." He got a cheer, and I approached the platform trying to think of some way to quieten the young hecklers sitting in the front row.

I started by saying that I always enjoyed good singing, and did they know "Home on the Range"? The laugh broke the ice, and I was able to continue with only minor disruptions.

As I expected, most of the students had never read the civil rights bill and didn't know that its passage meant the right of the central government to control numerous aspects of business, industry, and our personal lives. I quoted Lloyd Wright, a Los Angeles attorney and former president of the American Bar Association: "The civil rights aspect of this legislation is but a cloak. Uncontrolled federal executive power is the body. It is 10 per cent civil rights and 90 per cent extension of federal executive power."

By the time we arrived in Portland there was much speculation about my entry into the presidential primaries during 1964. My decision to run in the primaries was based on my desire to give the voters some alternative to the mad rush to federal control over our lives.

Thousands of persons had mailed their small contributions to help our cause, but we had no large donators and suffered from lack of financing. But I was determined to do the best with what we had.

What kind of people backed me? Concerned parents who wanted to preserve the neighborhood schools, homeowners wanting to protect their investment, union members wanting to protect their jobs and seniority, small businessmen who wanted to preserve the free-enterprise system, attorneys who believed in the Constitution, police officers who battled organized demonstrators in the streets, and all the little people who feared big government in the hands of phony intellectuals and social engineers with unworkable theories.

I sent Bill Jones to Madison in March to make the necessary arrangements to enter the Wisconsin primary in April. Mr. and Mrs. Lloyd Herbstreith began working day and night to meet the filing deadline of March 6. Their efforts got us several hundred signatures and we selected sixty for filing purposes.

We found many people reluctant in those days to offer their names as delegates. Later we were to understand the reason for their fears: they expected retaliation.

We got ballot position, and with little money and no campaign organization achieved amazing results against incredible odds. Pitted against us was the time factor, with only three weeks until the primary—and almost all the newspapers, reporters, radio, and television unsympathetic.

I decided to stick to basic issues. My offer to debate the civil rights bill with local politicians and clergymen had few takers. I opened my campaign in a climate as cool as the weather.

I could never bring myself to malign my opponents. I believe them to be mistaken, but I refuse to smear them or call them bigots or label them as demagogues. I believe that such usage serves only to throw a cloak of emotionalism over what should be honest debate.

Everywhere I went, I told my listeners that Congress was the only branch of the government that could stand against the onslaught of communism. It was my opinion that the judicial and executive branches could be taken over by subversives, but that Congress was more responsive to the people. "A Communist," I said, "hates the Congress, for the Congress is representative of the people. It is unwieldy. It has differing opinions. It is rampant with debate and deliberation—and most important, with truth. And communism cannot survive where there is truth."

I denounced lawmaking by executive or court edict. And I lashed out against the press for its eagerness to bury a public official with smearing propaganda. I pointed out that the civil rights bill placed "in the hands of a few men in central government the power to create a regulatory police arm unequaled in Western civilization."

Labor leaders had tried to misrepresent the civil rights bill, and I intended to let the rank-and-file membership know what its passage really meant. I pointed out that the federal government would be able to regulate their unions in hiring, firing, apprenticeship, and the time-honored practice of seniority. One power it would grant to the executive branch would be the right to establish ethnic quotas in hiring, rather than on a basis of merit or ability.

A member of a local union told me, "Governor, I am for you. I don't like too much government interference in my life."

During my stay in Kenosha, a militant picket tried to hit me with a sign. Jemison, my security guard, took the full blow on his head. The man who assaulted us was arrested on a disorderly conduct charge, found not guilty, and released.

If this had happened to, say, Adlai Stevenson in Dallas, the liberal press would have cried, "Shame," and pointed with alarm to the danger from the militant right. It was not easy to campaign in an atmosphere in which those who opposed us were granted complete license to disrupt and destroy my right to speak. The double standard was operating again.

During one of my speaking engagements, a reporter asked me, "Do you have an alternative to the civil rights bill?" This was an easy one. "Yes, sir, the U. S. Constitution. It guarantees civil rights to all the people, without violating the rights of anyone."

I closed an address in Appleton by saying, "If the people of Wisconsin want a civil rights bill for Wisconsin, let them enact it in their own state. That's the way it should be. But let's not have the federal government telling us what to do or what not to do."

In Milwaukee I told my delegates: "My campaign slogan when I was elected governor was 'Stand Up for Alabama.' Tonight I want to expand it to 'Stand Up for America!'"

That slogan became and remained the heart of my political and economic beliefs. The sacred oath of office that every elected official takes is to protect and defend the Constitution against all enemies, foreign and domestic. This concept of loyalty to the Constitution precludes any transfer of sovereignty to any international political body—which would be a treasonable violation of the supreme law of the land.

I believe George Washington would have had words to say about the civil rights bill and the growing power of the federal government. These words from his Farewell Address are significant today:

"It is important, likewise, that [leaders] should confine themselves within their respective Constitutional spheres, avoiding, in the exercise of the powers of one department, to encroach upon another. The spirit of encroachment tends to consolidate the powers of all departments in one, and thus to create, whatever the form of government, a real despotism."

Security was a constant consideration during our campaign. While we encountered friendly and enthusiastic supporters at the rallies, we had to contend with a small but militant group bent on disrupting them. After almost five weeks of being baited by the ignorant and threatened by the "non-violent" members of the "free speech" crowd, my nerves were frayed. I was so tired that I almost canceled what turned out to be the most enjoyable rally in Wisconsin.

Bill Jones had arranged for me to appear in South Milwaukee, getting the green light from the police for me to speak in the Serbian Memorial Hall. Thousands of Polish-Americans had come to hear me, and with them was a very fine band that kept playing "Way Down upon the Swanee River" over and over, to everyone's delight. Then, when we were least expecting anything new, the band struck up "Dixie," and three thousand or more voices sang "Dixie" in Polish. They never got beyond the first verse, but it certainly sounded good that cold night in South Milwaukee.

After my talk, I tried to shake hands with everyone in the hall. They had all been so friendly that I didn't want to leave. I remember that one fine-looking man grabbed me and said, "Governor, I have never been south of South Milwaukee, but I am a Southerner." Of course he was; the South is no longer geography —it's an attitude and a philosophy toward government.

God bless those wonderful, warm-hearted Americans from South Milwaukee! They help make political life rewarding and renew my faith in America.

When the votes were counted in Wisconsin, I had received 35 per cent. It was a highly rewarding result, taking into account the odds I had faced and the opposition of the professional politicians in Wisconsin.

I flew home to Alabama for a brief rest before going on to Indiana.

During my swing through Indiana I talked to the students at Butler University. I held high a copy of the civil rights bill and told them: "I advocate only that you decide for yourself. This says the civil rights program will be pushed down your throat by the social engineers in Washington, who will also tell you that the children of Indiana will have to be cross-transported to distant schools to achieve something they call 'ethnic balance.'"

By this time I was accustomed to the sameness of the questions asked by students. One of these was: "Are you concerned about the image you create abroad?" My answer: "It's about time we quit worrying about what they think of us and let them start worrying about what we think of them. It's our money they are spending. We don't have to apologize for America. We have more civil rights per square inch here than they have in a square mile behind the Iron Curtain."

I tried to amuse the audience by explaining the civil rights bill in abstract terms: "If you are a farmer employing Japanese Methodists, this bill can force you to hire some Chinese Baptists, because the bill says you can't discriminate because of race, religion, or national origin. This will not help labor, because it does not create one, single job. All it does is take your job and give it to someone else."

"One of the effects of this bill," I charged, "is to destroy the right of trial by jury. If your grandmother runs a boardinghouse and she is found guilty of discrimination under this bill, she can be sent to jail without a trial. How can it be a civil rights bill, when it destroys the most basic of all civil rights, that of trial by a jury of your peers?"

I decided to needle some of the liberal professors who would have denied me the right to speak on the campus. I made a plea to return to godliness in the nation. "I am not like all these pseudoliberals, who think their mind is the greatest thing on earth. I believe that God made us all and loves us all."

In a press conference at Butler University, I repudiated the "racist" label pinned on me by the left-wing, liberal press. One familiar question was asked: "What about all the federal aid Alabama receives—do you object to that kind of interference?"

I answered: "No one turns down federal aid if it is good. But actually we don't get any federal aid, because there is no such thing. It is taxpayers' aid, because it is your money and my money, and they just return a small portion to us after throwing most of it down a rathole somewhere."

The Democratic Party hierarchy was all out to defeat me in Indiana, and we ran into vicious personal attacks. But the May 5 primary gave me a surprising 30 per cent of the vote. Top labor leaders had waged a vigorous campaign against me, but in Hammond, Indiana, a strong union town, I defeated Governor Matthew Welsh by a small margin, causing the mayor of Hammond to remark, "It's a crying shame." Union support proved that the rank and file of union workers think and act independently.

During the course of the presidential primaries, I spoke before the National Press Club. The president of the club announced that I would not be presented with the traditional certificate of appreciation usually given to invited guests because "We don't like Governor Wallace's tactics."

Only a short time before, this same club had given certificates of appreciation to Fidel Castro and Nikita Khrushchev when they addressed this distinguished and unbiased body.

I remember saying at the time, "I suppose they like Khrushchev's and Castro's tactics. They are going to bury us, they have missiles aimed at us, they shoot our pilots down, and they represent a system that has brought more misery into the world than any yet known to man. The club leaders don't like my tactics but evidently approve of the tactics of dictators." Then I added, "As far as I am concerned, the National Press Club can take its traditional certificate—and they know what they can do with it."

Later they tried to soften the slight by saying I had not gotten the certificate because some newsman had been reported beaten to a pulp in Alabama. The story was false. The newsman alleged to have been beaten came into my office, without a scratch on him, an hour and a half after the incident was supposed to have taken place. More make-believe on the part of the media.

But if the National Press Club didn't care to hear about property rights, local government, and the Constitution, other Americans did. After addressing the University of Notre Dame, I made arrangements to appear before the House Judiciary Committee, which was then considering the prayer amendment to the U. S. Constitution. I testified on the same day as Bishop Fulton Sheen. I told the committee it was "fantastic" that the American people found it necessary to beseech Congress for restoration of their cherished right to have their children participate in a simple invocation at the beginning of a school day. "That right," I said, "has been nullified by the United States Supreme Court by a decree as sweeping and as deadly as any ever issued by any dictatorial power on the face of this earth." I added, "It is the bitter fruit of the liberal dogma that worships human intelligence and scorns the concept of divinity."

"When the crimes of humanity are finally catalogued," I concluded, "this monstrous breach of faith by the non-elected branch of government must stand out as one of history's great infamies."

I took time off from campaigning in Maryland to appear on the "Today" show on TV. Neil Boggs handled the program in the Washington studio, and Hugh Downs assisted him from New York. Downs introduced me and said, "The leaders of the Democratic Party are taking a different view of Alabama's Governor George C. Wallace than they did when he first started his three-state quest of the Democratic presidential nomination. He did not win in Indiana and Wisconsin, although he did register what even his opponents have termed a surprising showing. Now at hand is the Maryland primary, which Wallace himself calls the big one."

Boggs and I discussed the civil rights bill. I told him it was a grave issue that required more time and thought and should not be passed in a rush. He commented, "It has been a rather strange campaign in all three states. . . . You have campaigned against the bill, while candidates have been campaigning against you as an individual."

I answered, "They try to obscure the issues in the campaign. I'm not going to engage in personalities. I am in the state of Maryland as a guest, and for me to cast invective and to say hard things against any official of that state would be presumptuous on my part, because I am a guest. I think the issues are important and not personalities."

Boggs then asked me to identify the vociferous left-wing minority behind the civil rights bill and other domestic issues. I told him, "It's a group who feels that the central government can run our lives better than we can. And I say that the people who oppose this bill have been cowed into not speaking out, because of charges that you'd be a racist, or immoral, or a bigot, or prejudiced. Those are the people I am talking about; they're loud but they are not in the majority, although they are running this country to some extent."

Boggs mentioned that the civil rights bill had the support of President Johnson and many members of Congress, and asked if I considered them part of this group. I replied deliberately that I had no intention of impugning the motives of the President or any member of Congress. I then quoted President Johnson's views as a member of Congress on this same legislation: "I hope that the Senate is never seriously called upon to consider any such bill as this." I pointed out that when President Johnson was in the Senate he had even filibustered against the bill, calling it the worst bill ever brought before the U. S. Senate.

Downs challenged my statement that the bill affected the sale and rental of private homes, saying that it contained no provision whatever to that effect. I had to remind him that he was referring only to the section excluding bona fide private clubs, but that Title 6 did talk about homes. I pointed out that two former American Bar Association presidents had said that the bill validated executive orders of the President in the matter of housing in any part of the United States. "This is a tricky bill and it should be read very carefully, Mr. Downs."

Downs didn't want to give up, and once more read the section excluding application to private clubs or other non-public establishments. I had to clear that up once more. "Well, private clubs, that's a matter of Knights of Columbus, the Masonic Order, and so forth—but that's a very small part of American life. As far as privacy is concerned, this bill does affect your home and boardinghouses and beauticians and barbers and stenographers—it does affect every businessman in the United States, and every farmer, and every labor-union member and every school in the country."

Even when personal attacks became the most vicious, I refused to attack my opponents. The civil rights bill was the issue, and I had no intention of engaging in mudslinging. I was called a stumblebum, a liar, a phony, and some much stronger epithets.

Top labor leaders came to Maryland to denounce me. The rank and file of union members in Hammond and Gary, Indiana, had not listened to them, and I had carried those two industrial cities. They did not want this to happen in Maryland.

I enjoyed exhibiting a seventy-six-foot-long signed petition from union men in Alabama who from their hard-earned money had given one and two dollars each to help me. Rank-and-file workers knew that I was not anti-labor; this was evident in my record in the state legislature and as governor. Workingmen understand perfectly how the provisions of this bill would affect their seniority, their neighborhood schools, and open occupancy. Their world was not one of fantasies and illusions, but a daily encounter with hard, uncompromising reality.

Prior to the Maryland elections, I spoke to the students of the University of Maryland. It was a balanced mixture of pro and anti elements. I was frequently insulted and had a hard time keeping the opposing forces apart. I quieted the heckling for a while by saying, "I have always heard that the hallmark of a liberal is a willingness to hear the other side. Listen to me, and then if you don't agree, we will agree to disagree agreeably."

When protesters started giving out their moaning sounds, I would counter with, "Show that fellow where the boy's room is."

I still banged away at what the bill would do to every business, school, and individual in the United States, with the hope that some of the more curious students would take time to read the bill. As I expected, the bill was being debated in an atmosphere of slogans and emotional appeals. I seldom found any student who had read the bill who was in favor of it.

The only time my opponent, Senator Brewster, and I crossed paths was at the TV station, WBAL, when we were both using the station to make our addresses. Although I was a guest in his state and he should have made the initial gesture of greeting, I strode across the stage and held out my hand. "Senator Brewster, I am glad to see you again." Although portrayed as a genteel country gentleman, Brewster replied coldly, "I shake hands with you out of respect for the system that allows you to be in the state, but I don't respect you or your principles."

I bit my lip and turned around and went back to my seat

without replying. Perhaps there is truth to the saying that politics is no game for a gentleman.

I closed my campaign in Glen Burnie the night before election. I didn't have to put down the hecklers. Whenever an insult was hurled, some partisan fan in the audience would shout, "We love you, George," and everyone would start to clap.

The vote count proved it was my territory. In fewer than ten days of campaigning, against the combined strength of the Democratic Party, the prestige of the presidency, and out-of-state senators who supported Brewster, we had reaped an incredible 44 per cent of the popular vote.

A celebration was staged in Legion Hall the night of the election. The crowds cheered and yelled their approval as I grasped Lurleen's hand and held it high. When it came time to leave, it was almost impossible for Lurleen and me to make our way through the enthusiastic crowd. My security had more than a few moments of anxiety, because it is in this kind of situation that a candidate is most vulnerable—right in the middle of a loyal crowd.

Our showing in the three primaries made me regret not having entered more.

A few days after the Maryland primary, Senator Richard Russell told the Senate that the Wallace vote in Maryland would not defeat the civil rights bill in the Senate. "The Senate," he commented wryly, "is usually the last place in government to get the drift of American public opinion."

My office in Montgomery was flooded with letters supporting me and asking that I run for President even if it meant forming a new party. At that time we were confronted with a real problem just to get on the ballot in North Carolina.

To qualify for a ballot position in North Carolina, we had to be nominated by one of the two parties or to submit ten thousand signatures of qualified voters to the North Carolina Board of Elections. We had fewer than fifteen days to obtain the needed signatures, and the task was further complicated by the fact that each signature had to be certified before a state notary. The process was deliberately designed to make it difficult for independents to get on the ballot, and for a period of ten to fifteen years none had managed to do so.

Ed Ewing's plan was to organize forty teams, and it worked.

We obtained one hundred thousand signatures in less than two weeks (each signer, incidentally, paying a five-cent filing fee). By this time, there was no doubt about my grass-roots support.

In the meantime, however, I had been giving really hard thinking to whether or not to stay in the presidential race. On June 19, 1963, I appeared on CBS's "Face the Nation" and made my formal announcement of withdrawal as a candidate for the presidency in 1964. I pointed out that my purpose had been to "conservatize both national parties and to get a message to the leadership of both parties." States' rights had finally become a real issue in the election. I said that I felt my mission had been accomplished, thanked all those who had supported me, and bowed out.

As a result of canvassing nationally for new industry to locate in Alabama, the state enjoyed a record industrial growth. We had been so successful that I had to take on additional help in recruiting industry. During the early part of our speaking tours, Bill Jones had handled not only his heavy press-secretarial duties but had made all the arrangements for our meetings with industrial firms.

I asked Leonard Beard, of Alabama's Industrial Development Board, to assist us in setting up meetings with prospective firms, and to help him I chose retired Air Force Lieutenant General Walter E. Todd. The two did a splendid job in promoting new industry for Alabama.

To help finance promotion, the Alabama legislature appropriated two hundred thousand dollars, and from 1963 to 1965 industrial growth amounted to more than $1 billion. This new investment meant new jobs, plus an increase in income tax and sales tax revenues.

Wherever I went, I never missed an opportunity to speak about the economic future of Alabama. Increase in jobs would obviously benefit both races, and the additional state revenue would enable us to spend more on education. Our educational budget went up from 145 million in 1963 to 232 million in 1965. in four years we built twenty-nine junior colleges and trade schools. We were able to provide free textbooks for public school students through the twelfth grade.

This was all highly gratifying, because I am convinced that if our form of government is to work, it must have a broad base of literacy, and I wanted all the people of Alabama to benefit from increased educational opportunities.

Alabama, of course, remained a relatively poor state. But we had established solid agricultural and industrial bases for future economic growth.

Selma, Alabama, is situated in the heart of the "Black Belt," so called because of its rich black soil, which grows some of Alabama's finest cotton. In the years before the Civil War, cotton planters and brokers had grown rich in this region. The prominent Lehman family of New York traces its family fortune to Selma during the 1850s.

Selma is a quiet, peaceful town with many fine ante-bellum houses, churches, and one of Alabama's oldest synagogues.

Selma stopped being peaceful in early January 1965. This community of thirty thousand was subjected to mass demonstrations, sit-ins, and street marching. More than two thousand amateur and professional agitators and demonstrators kept the town's small police force on constant alert. Police and city officials were taxed to their human limits.

National TV networks, sensing that what was happening in Selma was "good show biz," produced daily live-action melodrama, without too much news objectivity. The news manipulators made it the "good guys versus the bad guys" in the best Western tradition.

The alleged motive for the protests and demonstrations was that the city was not integrating its public facilities fast enough. Later, when the date for the passage of the 1965 voting rights bill was approaching, Alabama voting laws were included in the list of grievances.

Selma had very recently elected a young, energetic, and capable new mayor, Joe Smitherman. After the passage of the 1964 Civil Rights Acts, Smitherman made plans to integrate quickly and smoothly the hotels, motels, theaters, and restaurants in Selma, in compliance with the act's desegregation provisions.

During this period of charged emotions, I extended the period for registration of eligible voters an additional ten days in December. Curiously, only twenty-six Negroes came in to register. I would have extended the period again, but under Alabama law no additional extensions were permitted.

For eight weeks the demonstrators tied up traffic, harassed

business houses, and kept the police on twenty-four-hour alert. Imagine New York City if suddenly seven hundred thousand people took to the streets to demonstrate and outsiders were sent in to make a Roman carnival out of it for telecasting.

Flooding the town were rare specimens of humanity: well-groomed young theologians, idealistic students, hippies looking for a cause and excitement, and professional agitators carrying out their assignments. Some of the demonstrators had long police records, a few had proven Communist affiliations—and most taunted the police with insults and profanity.

Despite the baiting and being spat upon by a new breed of barbarians, the police for the most part conducted themselves with exemplary restraint. Then came the fateful confrontation between the marchers and the troopers east of Pettus Bridge in early March.

I believe it was Napoleon who said, "History is a legend agreed upon." Before this event is forgotten and the legend agreed upon, I would like to tell Alabama's side of the story.

Martin Luther King announced on March 3, 1965, that he would lead a march from Selma to Montgomery on Highway 80. This compelled me as governor of Alabama to decide whether or not to allow the march, taking into consideration the safety of the marchers and the rights of all Alabamians.

On Thursday, March 4, I called an urgent meeting of my staff, along with the director of public safety, Al Lingo, and his staff. We discussed ways and means to protect the marchers with our limited state troopers and local police agencies. The meeting lasted several hours, without producing any final decision.

Bill Jones finally came up with a plan that seemed feasible and would allow the march to take place without any risk of death or injury from motor vehicles. Highway 80 would be closed to all motor traffic between Selma and Montgomery. The march would be allowed but for foot traffic only. In previous marches, the leaders had often ridden while the rank and file of their sympathizers had walked. Sleeping trailers would not be allowed on the highway.

To make certain that I had the support of the legislators from the counties where the march would take place, I called them to my office to ask their opinion. Most thought the plan was good, but a few, along with representative Bill Edward of Lowndes

County, objected strongly. Edwards felt, and rightly, that the heavily wooded areas in his county would provide tempting cover for extremists to shoot at the marchers, or worse yet, to plant explosives along the way.

I called back Lingo, Major John Cloud, and Major William Jones. We discussed the problem and made our decision to stop the march. We agreed that troopers would be stationed across the highway east of Edmund Pettus Bridge and would halt the march at that point. Under no circumstances were the troops to advance against the marchers. They had orders to raise their nightsticks in a manner if the marchers continued to move forward after having been given orders to halt. If necessary, the troopers were to fall back and use tear gas to disperse the crowd. I wanted no tragedies, either intentional or accidental, and I gave firm orders to use minimal force.

I called a press conference the following morning and announced our decision and the reasons why it was taken. I learned that Martin Luther King had been detained in Atlanta and would not be able to get to Selma for the march scheduled for Sunday. I went to bed that night convinced that only a routine demonstration would take place on Sunday.

Tension was high as the demonstrators started toward Pettus Bridge, led by Hosea Williams, from Atlanta, Georgia. The marchers came closer and closer to the troopers, finally stopping perhaps a hundred feet from them.

Major Cloud shouted over his bullhorn, "Turn around and go back to your church. You will not be allowed to march any further."

The marchers started to move ahead. Cloud told them they were an unlawful assembly. "If you disperse, you will be allowed to return freely to town. You have two minutes."

At the end of the two-minute period, the troopers moved into the waiting demonstrators with their clubs swinging and kept driving into the crowd after the tear gas was fired. As Major Cloud tells the story, he gave no orders to attack, and because of the noise of the melee it was almost impossible to hear commands. When it was over, there were mercifully no serious injuries—and no deaths. But this was not at all the way I had wanted things to turn out. I was saddened and angry.

As expected, the full righteous wrath of the nation's press, television, and radio were directed against Alabama and its governor. Not once did the press say, "If the marchers had obeyed a lawful order, this awful thing would not have happened."

Los Angeles was to suffer bloody and destructive riots in the fall of 1965, but even though thirty-nine people died, no reflecton was made on the governor by the nation's press.

Editorial writers had an orgiastic field day at the expense of guiltless people in my state. The press, thousands of miles away from the events, portrayed me as a vicious, brutal, and heartless man. What had happened pained me deeply, but in my heart and conscience I knew I had tried my best to prevent any clash between the troopers and the marchers.

The Washington *Post* wrote: "Congress . . . must promptly pass legislation that will put into federal hands the registration of voters. . . ."

The New York *Herald Tribune* came close to the truth when it wrote: "Just as the troubles in Birmingham brought about the Civil Rights Act of 1964, [Selma] is almost certain to bring about the Civil Rights Act of 1965."

The Chattanooga *News-Free Press* wrote: "King's crowd did not really want to get to Montgomery. They wanted an incident. They got it."

King renewed his pledge to march to Montgomery. In a surprising move, Federal Judge Johnson, my old adversary, issued a temporary injunction forbidding King and his followers to march. But King decided to go ahead with his plans in violation of federal-court orders. My troopers were ordered back to the bridge, with instructions to give way if marchers persisted in moving ahead. This time I knew the troopers would avoid any clash.

At the confrontation, Federal Marshall H. Stanley Fountain asked the marchers to halt. He read part of the court order forbidding the march. King told him, "I am aware of the court order." King and his followers moved ahead, to be stopped once more by troopers under Al Lingo's vigilance.

When King least expected it, the line of troopers parted, leaving the highway wide open to Montgomery. But King and his followers turned around and marched back to church.

After consulting with my advisers, I sent a telegram to President Johnson asking for a meeting with him to discuss the demonstrations in Alabama.

Just prior to my departure for Washington, protesters had obtained a permit to demonstrate in Montgomery. They did so, far into the night. The permit had a 6-P.M. limit, but they kept it up until well past midnight. Then a rain began to fall and they broke up. But before leaving, about 150 of the hard-core demonstrators performed a mass urination on Dexter Avenue.

My conference with President Johnson at the White House on March 12, 1965, lasted more than three hours. The President was warm and cordial, and we covered a wide range of subjects during our frank conversations.

President Johnson was as anxious to end the demonstrations in Selma as I was. He felt that King should be allowed to make the march, and he believed that once the 1965 voting rights bill was passed, the demonstrations would stop. I could not accept his premise in this matter, because I felt that once "street revolutions" succeed, there is no end to this method of gaining political objectives.

I told the President the fifty-mile route from Selma to Montgomery went through heavily wooded areas that would make security measures difficult. My fear was that some thug or *provocateur* might shoot at the marchers or commit some other violence. I informed the President that Alabama's resources in manpower and money could be better used to help our citizens than dissipated in guarding the march. I assured him that even though I was opposed to the march, I would do everything within my power to provide for the marchers' safety.

The President was of course in favor of the civil rights legislation he had sponsored in 1964, and he was pressing for the enactment of the voting rights bill in 1965 to end control of voting requirements by the states. I explained that many of my objections to the takeover of state functions by the federal government were the same objections he had expressed when he was a member of Congress. He answered me by saying that he was still against the federal government's telling industry how to hire and fire their employees. We differed less in our goals than in the methods to achieve them within the constitutional system.

On several occasions I made an effort to leave, not wanting to impose on the President's time. But each time I tried to end the meeting, the President would say, "Goerge, we aren't through yet —we have more to talk about."

Then he confided, "Governor, some of the people who used to oppose me are now my biggest supporters since I changed my stand. Times are changing, and we have to change with them."

The President believed in universal suffrage without any qualifying conditions. Everyone should vote without discrimination because of race, color, or creed. I told him I was also for non-discrimination, but under the Constitution the states should establish the voting conditions. My position was that a person unable to read and write impairs and lowers the standard of political life. How could an illiterate vote intelligently in an increasingly complex world? The answer, in my opinion, was to make education available to all our citizens and not to lower qualitative standards. Any test should be non-prohibitive and should be administered on an equal and non-discriminatory basis. "Mr. President, if I endorsed your views on suffrage, I could not return to Alabama and face my people."

I pointed out that the voting rights bill was so cleverly worded that it applied to only five states: Alabama, South Carolina, Louisiana, Georgia, and Mississippi. In those states an illiterate is allowed to vote, but if that same illiterate moved to New York he could not vote, because he is illiterate. And that, I said, is rank discrimination.

I went on record as saying that in some few counties in Alabama discrimination had taken place, but Negroes meeting Alabama's voting conditions were voting, and their numbers were increasing all the time. What the President and Congress were doing was to destroy the constitutional system, and the cure would produce more evils than the illness.

After more than three hours of open and frank conversation, the President invited me to accompany him to his press conference. "Come on, George," he said, grabbing me by the arm, "let's meet the press."

Reporters were pushing and shoving trying to get close to the President, and I tried to stay a respectful distance behind. He wouldn't have it that way. "Come on, George, let's go together." I mounted the podium with him, and the President very graciously introduced me. I spoke briefly about the nature of our talks, without referring to any of the private matters discussed.

The press conference over, I went to the airport and returned home.

In Montgomery, I spoke on ABC's "Issues and Answers" in a live telecast of a press conference. I was pleased that Murphy Martin would appear on the program. Martin had always been fair with me. I never knew or cared whether he agreed with me, but I did appreciate his objectivity. I told the television audience what I would do if Judge Johnson should give an order permitting Martin Luther King and his group to march to Montgomery.

I made it clear I would obey even a court order I didn't like, in contrast with the attitude of the demonstrators, who insisted on having their way regardless of what the law and the courts say. King's theory was that there are two kinds of law—just and unjust. He had gone ahead and marched toward Pettus Bridge in violation of a federal court order. (Judge Johnson later made a curious ruling that King had not defied the court order—no wonder the man in the street has little faith in courts.)

As we all expected, Judge Johnson ruled on March 17 that King could have his march. His ruling gave the marchers everything they had asked for, plus requiring Alabama to provide for their safety. Acknowledging the burden on Alabama's law enforcement agencies, Johnson added to his ruling, "The U. S. Government stands ready . . . to assist in providing police protection for this proposed march."

I was served with the court order the following day. That night, I spoke to a joint session of the Alabama legislature, asking them to adopt a record educational budget.

I asked the Department of Public Safety to determine what would be needed in the way of manpower and transportation to insure the safety of the marchers and still have adequate protection for the people of Alabama. The report was disheartening. Alabama would have to mobilize sixty-five hundred troopers, police, and guardsmen to handle security for an expected thirty-thousand marchers and supporters. In addition to the manpower requirements, we would need six ambulances, mobile aid stations, portable toilets, and trucks. The cost of this walkathon would be paid out of the public treasury, despite the fact that most Alabamians—black and white—were opposed to the march.

The federal judge had set the guidelines, the President of the

United States had given his blessing to the marchers, King and his followers had written the script, and Alabama would pick up the tab for the telecasted spectacle. We had lost the battle. But I was allowed to make the final move.

Article 4, section 4, of the United States Constitution gave me the answer. I immediately dispatched a telegram requesting federal troops be sent to Alabama to guarantee the march that the federal court had ordered. That night, I spoke to the joint houses of the Alabama legislature, asking them to pass a resolution asking for federal troops. I told the legislature it would cost from $350,000 to $400,000 to police the march. "The federal courts have created this situation," I said. "They can help us out of it."

That night, the Alabama legislature unanimously passed a resolution requesting federal troops be sent to Alabama. News accounts reported that the President was furious because of the short notice of our request. But the march was scheduled to begin in two days, and Alabama was expected to make short-notice preparations.

The irony was obvious: a year before, Alabama received troops without asking for them. Now that the request had been made constitutionally, the President reluctantly complied.

The long-heralded march began Sunday, March 21, 1966. Five thousand people left Selma, crossed Pettus Bridge, and headed east on Highway 80.

Walking with Martin Luther King were John Lewis, national chairman of the Student Non-violent Coordinating Committee; comedian Dick Gregory (who was later wounded in the riots in the Watts district of Los Angeles), and a host of noted civil rights leaders. Behind King came hundreds of ministers, hundreds of reporters, thousands of soldiers, scores of federal agents and marshals. Circling overhead were press and television cameramen in army helicopters. The marchers walked along the right two lanes of the four-lane highway. The left two lanes handled auto traffic. The elite and their followers covered seven and a half miles that day.

Sleeping quarters to accommodate the marchers consisted of two brown tents set up in campsites—one for women and one for men. A large green tent was used for meetings and eating. Powerful army generators heated the tents on chilly nights. Military security was tightened at night.

For two more days and nights the marchers plodded on to Montgomery, their numbers reduced to three hundred by court order when they entered the two-lane section of Highway 80. On hand to meet the tired marchers were King and more than five thousand supporters. King had left the march earlier to fly to Cleveland for a speaking engagement.

That night, on the baseball field at St. Jude's High School, the marchers staged a New York-Hollywood star-studded super production rivaling anything ever seen before in Alabama. The star performers included Sammy Davis, Jr.; Peter, Paul and Mary; Leonard Bernstein; Dick Gregory; Harry Belafonte; Shelley Winters, Ina Balin, and many others. The floodlights were provided by Maxwell Air Force Base.

Alabamians and their governor were the butt of many imported jokes that night. The majority of Alabamians ignored the whole thing.

It was a great personal relief when the demonstrations and parades ended without a single incident that could provide the national press with a pretext for pillorying Alabamians. I had told the people of Alabama to leave the marchers alone. "Don't pay any attention to insults from agitators. Avoid the marchers and stay off the streets." The real heroes of the march were the average citizens of Alabama, black and white, who remained calm and peaceful despite strong provocation from many of the agitators.

Then came the lamentable aftermath. Not one incident had marred the march, but while returning to Selma from Montgomery a Mrs. Liuzzo from Detroit was shot and killed. I told the press that night: "The murder was tragic. Life simply should not be that cheap." Nothing could have made me sadder than this senseless shooting, after all our efforts to prevent this sort of thing from happening.

The shooting took place in Lowndes County, the very county that State Representative Bill Edwards had said was too dangerous for the marchers to cross. The news wolves naturally set up a howl, pointing the finger at me. I was no more responsible for the shooting of Mrs. Liuzzo than Governor Rockefeller was for the death of Malcolm X in New York, or Governor Reagan for the killings in Watts, or the governor of Michigan for riots in his state.

The men arrested for the shooting had not come from Lowndes County, but from Jefferson County, eighty miles away.

Two days later, the whole unpleasant episode was behind us.

Several days after the demonstrators had left Montgomery, I met with a delegation of sixteen petitioners—fifteen black and one white—all residents of the state of Alabama. It gave me great pleasure to meet again attorney Fred Gray of Montgomery, who was one of the petitioners. We began what I believe was a frank and fruitful discussion of our points of view. Their petition had to do principally with voting rights, and I restated my position that eligible Negroes should have the same right to vote as anyone else.

I told them it was important that we have an informed electorate in our complex age, and that education for all in Alabama would answer many of the problems. I pointed out that since becoming governor I had increased teacher salaries more than 29 per cent and that the Negro teacher's salary was slightly higher than that of the white teacher.

I directed my next remarks to Dr. Foster, President of Tuskegee Institute. "Dropouts are the main problem we have in Alabama in educating members of the Negro race. This problem must be solved. We have to keep these children in school, because if they drop out in the second and third grade, then ten years later they can't get a job because they are not trained for any type of work, and thus they must get relief to have food and money. I am working so that every student can have free textbooks, and this will eliminate the problem of books for our poorer students."

I outlined what the twenty-nine junior colleges and trade schools would mean to all our citizens. I mentioned that the promotion of new industry for the state had created some twenty-six thousand jobs for Negro workers.

I mentioned my service on the board of trustees of Tuskegee and my constant efforts to get larger appropriations for the school. And I added that Tuskegee received about three quarters of a million dollars from the Alabama legislature, an amount almost equal to the cost of servicing and protecting the marchers.

One of the petitioners interrupted me. "Governor, you certainly talk convincingly, and if I don't get out of here soon, you will have me persuaded that you are completely right." I laughed and went on to another point of their petition, police brutality.

I told them that my orders to the state police were to use only the minimum force necessary at any time to handle demonstrations or marches. "But I must say this to you: When these men are on duty day and night for numbers of weeks, it becomes increasingly difficult for them to stay in good humor. They are humans. They like to be at home, not out handling demonstrations and marchers. And let me say this: even the Justice Department has complimented the Alabama state police, saying that with one or two exceptions they have acted with restraint."

I went back to the matter of voter registration: "I gave the Dallas [Selma] County Board of Registrars ten extra days early this year, and do you know that only twenty-six Negroes showed up in that time? Yet when the demonstrations started, there were so many clogging the rooms and disrupting the registration process that it was almost impossible to register anyone. We have to use a little sense in these matters."

I closed by saying, "Let me say that never in my life have I made any speech that reflected on any man because of his race, color, or creed or national origin."

The meeting ended, and I had benefited from this opportunity to exchange ideas with fellow Alabamians. One of the petitioners, a Mr. Lowry, was quoted as saying after the meeting, "We were received cordially and courteously by the governor. I hope it will prove fruitful in building bridges of communications."

MILLION-DOLLAR LADY

I was pleased with the progress made in Alabama during my first term as governor. The state's industrial growth was outstanding. Hundreds of new industries had created new jobs for our citizens. Increased revenue from corporate taxes enabled the state to undertake ambitious school, hospital, and road programs.

Equally satisfying was the fact that the political movement begun in Alabama to save the Constitution and preserve local government had expanded into a national crusade.

I realized that the only hope to continue my programs in Alabama and stay alive in the national movement was to find some way to seek re-election in 1966. Alabama law did not allow a governor to succeed himself. Loss of my political power base in Alabama could mean the end of my national political career.

I requested the legislature to pass a bill providing for a statewide referendum allowing the voters to decide whether or not a governor should be allowed to seek re-election. I believed the democratic way was to let the people decide the issue. The bill failed to pass the legislature.

Chafing a bit from my legislative defeat, I said half in jest during an informal press conference, "I might just run my wife in 1966." This off-the-cuff remark later prompted Lurleen's decision to run as my stand-in.

As the filing deadline drew near, I became convinced Lurleen could win. Nevertheless, I hesitated to ask her, because of her recent cancer surgery. In January, at St. Margaret's Hospital, she had undergone a hysterectomy, an appendectomy, and a thorough abdominal exploration to make certain no malignancy was left.

The doctors were optimistic about Lurleen's long-term health outlook. She made such a rapid recovery that we gave the matter little more thought.

One day I asked Lurleen, "Would you agree to run for governor?" She replied without hesitation, "Yes, George, I will." Then she added in a matter-of-fact way, "But let me check with the doctors before we make any definite decision."

Lurleen's physicians expressed the view that she was able to stand the rigors of a gubernatorial campaign—and in fact that involvement in politics would be good therapy for her. I still had lingering doubts, however. One day, after several especially exasperating hours in the office, I returned to the mansion determined to return to private law practice in Clayton after my term ended. "We are not going to run! This job is hard enough on a strong man, let alone a woman. Let's go home to Clayton and have time for ourselves and our children."

Lurleen would have none of that. "George, we are going to run. We can stand up to the pressures you mention. I want to run!" Then she added gently, "I'll be disappointed if I can't."

My political enemies have accused me of forcing my wife to run. The truth is what I told Holmes Alexander shortly after Lurleen's death. "Allow me to dissolve one of the cruder lies that has gone out of Alabama. My wife was not dragooned cat's-paw into becoming governor. She loved every minute of being governor the same way and for the same reasons Margaret Smith loves being a United States senator."

During the next few months, I watched in amazement as Lurleen made the transformation from unpretentious wife and mother into capable political campaigner. I was really proud of her. In those months we grew closer from shared experience. Looking back, I think those months were the happiest of our lives.

Lurleen appeared before the television cameras to announce her candidacy on the night of February 24, 1966. "I am happy today to offer the voters of Alabama the opportunity of enjoying continued progress, prosperity, and the honest, efficient government that has been so much in evidence during my husband's administration."

The campaign was on.

Dressed in a neat blue blazer and white skirt, Lurleen traveled across the state, gaining confidence as she went. At first she made minispeeches, while I handled the longer ones. Our "Ma and Pa" campaign became the "Alabama Movement." I told the audiences, "Elect my wife governor and we will continue the fight against the federal courts and big government." I hinted early that if no one was acceptable to me, I might just become a presidential candidate in 1968.

Early in the campaign, I came down with the flu. On her own, Lurleen had to make longer speeches and learn to ad-lib. The primary campaign had so many candidates that I did not see how a run-off could be avoided. I sat with little Lee watching the returns on election night. Lee kept looking in amazement as the votes were tabulated on the blackboard. "Daddy," she said, "are all those figures for Mama?"

There was no need for a run-off. Lurleen had received 480,841 votes, a clear majority. She now faced a general election against the strongest Republican candidate in many years, Jim Martin.

Following Lurleen's victory, we took a family vacation on the Gulf Coast. We fished, swam, and lay on the beach. We didn't know it at the time, but it was to be our last vacation together.

We stuck to the same style and the same issues in the general election campaign. Lurleen had become a surprisingly polished speaker. She hit the local issues and I spoke out more and more on national issues. It was during my wife's campaign that the slogan was born: "There's Not a Dime's Worth of Difference" in the national presidential candidates.

I promised the voters in Alabama that if my wife was elected and if there was no change in the national parties' platforms, I would become a presidential candidate in 1968.

Lurleen wound up her campaign in Clayton. Before a crowd estimated at nine thousand, she made some simple and sincere promises: "We will not quit our beliefs for fleeting popularity. We will not sacrifice our principles for the praise of editors. . . . We will stand up for Alabama—and for America!"

Lurleen won with 537,505 votes to Jim Martin's 262,942. She had received the most votes ever given to a gubernatorial candidate in Alabama history.

I'm sure part of her success was due to her sincere and concerned manner of speaking. She could charm crowds with her ladylike manner and warm personality. I was immensely proud of her, and it didn't hurt a bit to take a back seat to her in vote-getting ability.

There were many quips about the election victory. NBC's "Today" show came out with "The governor of Alabama is a mother." More than once I heard "Behind every successful woman candidate is a good man." Bob Hope quipped, "Governor Wallace deserves an Oscar for the 'Best Supporting Role of the Year.'" I even received a letter addressed: "He lives with Mrs. Wallace in the Governor's Mansion."

The cynics, of course, thought that Lurleen would be just a rubber stamp for me as governor. They didn't know her very well. We did agree on most things, but I soon found out that Lurleen had strong ideas and independence, although I was her most trusted adviser.

Lurleen was sworn in as governor on January 16, 1967, following a parade surpassing my own extravaganza in 1963. Dressed in a black cashmere dress, a pillbox hat, Lurleen was obviously happy. The day was a comfortable 55 degrees, and an estimated two hundred thousand people turned out for the parade and inauguration.

She stood poised and dignified in the cool afternoon air while Justice Livingston administered the oath of office. We had four special guests from Alabama, all winners of the Congressional Medal of Honor. I believe Alabama had seventeen medal holders, more per capita than any other state in the Union.

With us also were six of my World War II B-29 crew and their wives: George Harbinson of Mooresville, North Carolina; Richard Zind of Stamford, Connecticut; Robert Lamb of Louisville, Kentucky; Jason Riley of Columbia, South Carolina; and George Leahy of Norwich, Connecticut.

My old buddies told Lurleen, "George often talked about being governor someday, but we never thought his wife would [illegible], too."

[illegible]urleen defied tradition by canceling the inaugural ball in [illegible]tt Coliseum. She did not want to waste money on the ball [illegible]here was a war going on in Vietnam. She made a formal [illegible]t to the press saying, "I could not enjoy merrymaking [illegible]rican servicemen are risking their lives in Vietnam. I [illegible]oney spent for an inaugural ball wasted. Instead I dedicate this day and evening of my inauguration to our soldiers in Vietnam."

This was no grand play to the political bleachers. It came from the heart of a person incapable of being frivolous in time of war.

One of Lurleen's first acts as governor was to visit the Bryce State Mental Hospital, near Tuscaloosa. She vowed to do something to help those poor patients in that overcrowded and rundown hospital. On the same trip she also visited the Partlow State Hospital for mentally retarded children. She later told me, "George, I nearly broke into tears when a pathetic little child grabbed me and said, 'Mama!' "

A short time later, Lurleen called a special session of the legislature and pressed for a fifteen-million-dollar bond issue for reforms in mental-health and mental-retardation programs. She signed into law this piece of legislation just before leaving for Houston to start cobalt treatments. She always regarded this as her proudest accomplishment as governor.

Lurleen's tastes and habits suffered no change as governor. She still preferred small, inexpensive cars. "I developed my taste in cars," she explained jokingly, "when George and I could afford only a small, inexpensive car. We bought cars we could make the payments on."

In clothes, Lurleen liked chic, tailored dresses and suits with simple lines. She was never much for frills and pretentious fashions.

She disliked people who were false, affected, or presumptuous. When speaking to members of her cabinet, she would tell them, "Please say what you mean around me—and mean what you say." Because she was gentle by nature, she never liked rude or pushy people—and she had an uncanny eye for spotting phonies and opportunists.

The first six months of Lurleen's term in office were full of accomplishments. Her health was good and she found little time t spare. She then learned to understand why I had been av from the family so much.

After four months on the job, Lurleen took her summer tion at the Governor's Summer Mansion on Alabama shores, accompanied by Lee and her close friend, Steinecker. Early June was her favorite time of the loved to walk along the beach looking at the sea,

13. The brand-new legislator, 1947.

14. A young legislator addresses the American Legion.

15. The famous apron photo: George C. Wallace joins Governor Lurleen's kitchen cabinet—1967. Phillip Hamm watches.

16. New start. The entire family sits for a formal portrait right after my inauguration. The young people are (back): Peggy Sue (now Mrs. Mark Kennedy); George, Jr.; and Bobbie Jo's husband, Jim Parsons. At left, Jim Snively sits in front of his brother, Josh. In front of Cornelia is my youngest, Lee, and Bobbie Jo is holding Jason Corley Parsons on her lap

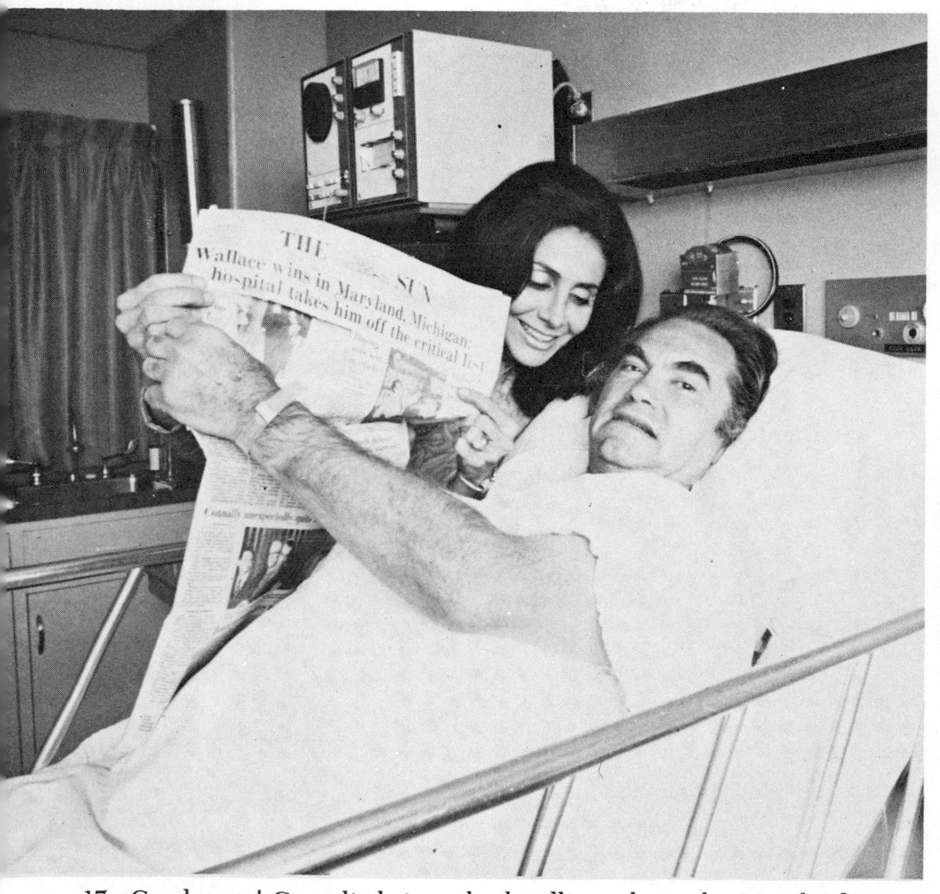

17. Good news! Cornelia brings the headlines about the Maryland and Michigan primaries.

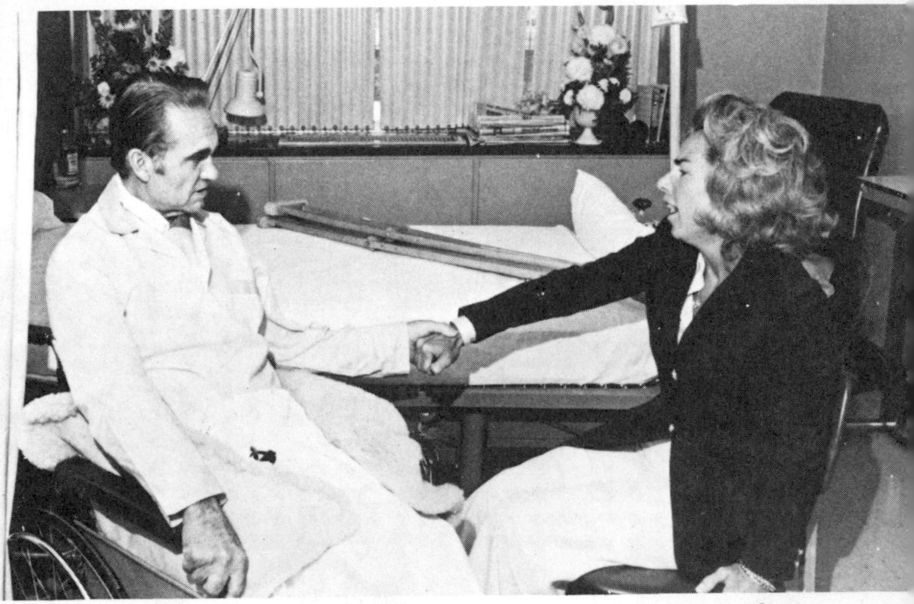

18. Ethel Kennedy's sympathy and encouragement were much appreciated.

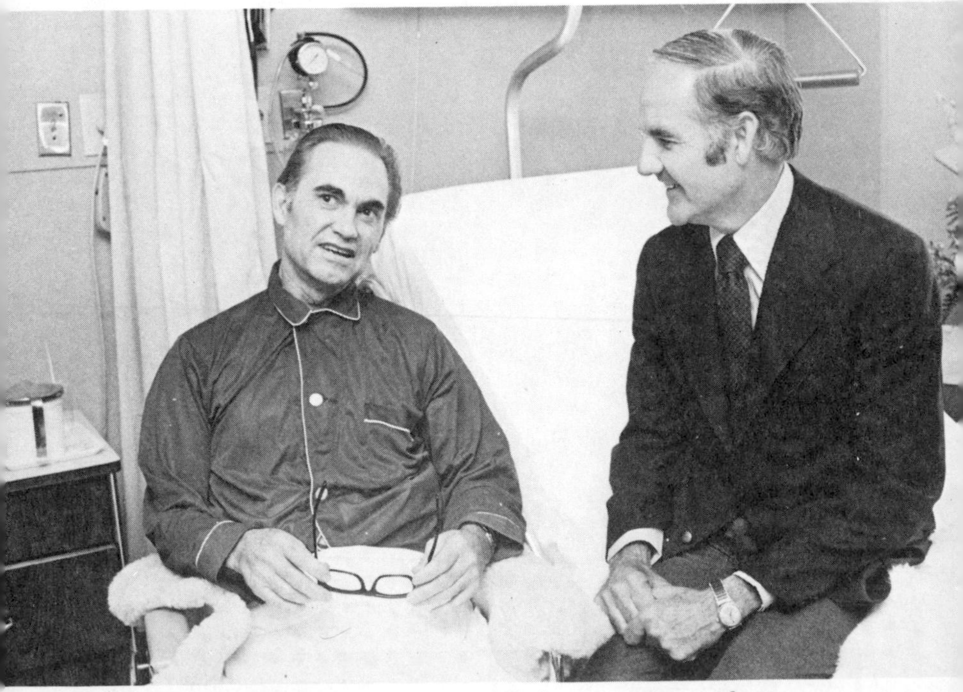

19. Senator McGovern visits me at Holy Cross Hospital.

20. Cornelia joins me at the hospital's dinner in my honor seven weeks after the shooting. Sister Helen Marie stands next to me.

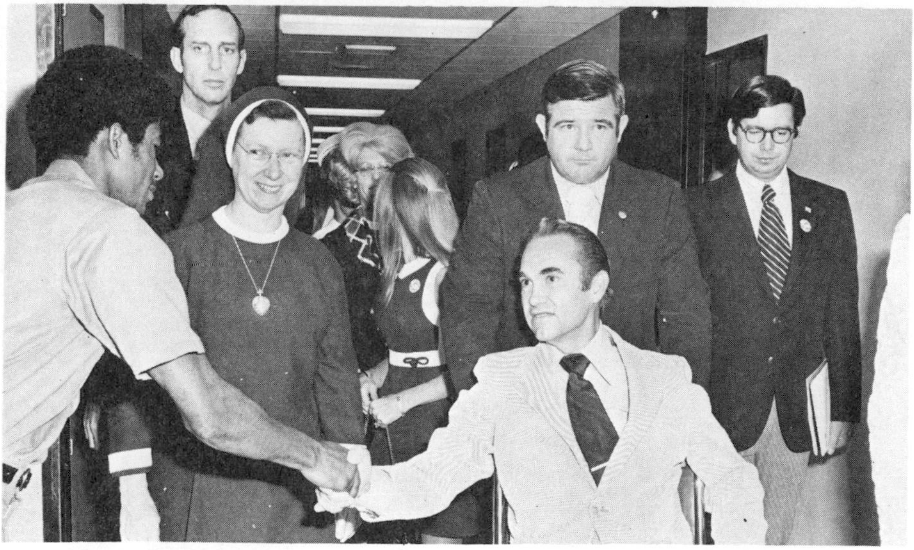

21. A farewell handshake from a hospital employee as we leave for the Miami Democratic Convention. Sister Helen Marie smiles approval, E. C. Dothard helps me with the wheelchair, and Billy Joe Camp is alongside. Jim Taylor of the Secret Service looks on. (Reni Photos)

22. At a reception I gave for the delegates to the Miami convention before it opened. In white suit is Billy Joe Camp. Standing behind me is Assistant Press Secretary Elvin Stanton, and at my left is Lieutenant Governor Jere Beasley.

the white summer clouds. For two golden weeks, she managed to forget the cares of office.

Then came the intense stomach pains. The doctors had doubled her hormone dosage just before the pains began. Perhaps this would explain them? But, remembering her cancer operation a short sixteen months before, she was frightened. Deceptively, the pains eased and disappeared.

Lurleen made frequent calls to me in Montgomery to tell me how wonderful the short vacation was. She enjoyed the trip to Fort Morgan, the exciting Creole food in Bon Secour, the fishing trips with Catherine's son, and the quiet nights on the beach talking to Lee about the sea. But before returning to Montgomery, she said ominously to Catherine Steinecker, "I won't be here a year from now."

Shortly after her return from the seacoast, the pains began again—this time more intense than before. Her physicians in Montgomery decided she needed new surgery and recommended a world-famous cancer clinic in Houston. This was the beginning of a seemingly endless series of tests, treatments, and surgery. After each operation, she rallied briefly, gained weight, and appeared to be recovering. But each time she suffered a relapse.

Her frail body was stocked with courage. She never lost her will to live, even when her body was ravaged by cancer. While waiting for the results of the numerous tests conducted at Anderson Hospital, she and I took in a baseball game at the Astrodome, ate at Trader Vic's with friends, or leisurely toured the city of Houston.

Lurleen's room was deluged with letters and cables wishing her a speedy recovery. Once, with a mischievous grin on her face she told one of the nurses, "Now, if you should happen to run across a letter for George in all this, just put it in a little pile over there." It was good to know that she didn't intend to crawl into a shell and become morose.

One day, a little old man came to the hospital office with a dozen yellow roses for Lurleen. He was at the point of tears when he could not find a place in the flower-laden room for his roses. Lurleen was touched when he asked, "Don't you have anyplace to put these roses, miss? They're for Guv'nuh Wallace."

Although Lurleen disliked being in a hospital, she felt this one was different. Everyone—patients and staff—seemed to be genuinely concerned. I believe I acted like any worried husband does when his wife is seriously ill. I sought reassurances from the doctors that my wife was getting well, and I asked her—probably much too often—how she was feeling.

Despite her never-failing sense of humor and faith in God, she was under no illusions about her condition. She resigned herself to face a serious operation on July 10. Dr. Robert Lee Clark, along with three personal physicians from Montgomery, spent more than four hours in surgery with Lurleen. They removed a malignant growth the size of an egg, along with ten inches of her colon. Fortunately, a colostomy was not necessary.

The cancer had not spread and the doctors were hopeful that it had been arrested and that Lurleen might whip the disease after all. But their hopes were short-lived.

After reaching home in Montgomery, Lurleen gained back five pounds. The doctors, to be on the safe side, sent her back to Anderson Hospital for radiation treatment in September. She dreaded this, because it usually brought on side effects of pain and nausea, especially when the cobalt rays were aimed at the abdominal region.

We took a two-bedroom apartment across from the hospital. As the cobalt treatments required only a few minutes a day, we had time to see the sights in Houston, visit with friends and family, and on weekends Lurleen flew home to be with the children.

After several weeks of radiation treatment, intense pain and nausea returned. Even when she was most severely afflicted, Lurleen kept up the front that she was all right. "I'm feeling fine, just fine," was her usual reply when asked how she was feeling. She resisted the idea of going to bed to rest, probably because she felt that as long as she stayed on her feet, things weren't too bad. No matter how excruciating the pains became, she didn't want to call the hospital.

We finally had to compel her to go back. She was given glucose, because she couldn't keep food down. She was losing weight and was too weak to continue with radiation treatments. After a few days in the hospital, she bounced back sufficiently to enable us to drive back to Montgomery, with a stopover in New Orleans.

Once home, Lurleen had several weeks without pain. But just when she felt she was recovering, the pains hit her again—this time from a new cancer in her pelvic area.

I was out in California working desperately to get on the California ballot for my presidential bid in 1968. This meant a struggle to get sixty-six thousand California voters to sign up in the American Independent Party.

Without any previous notice, Lurleen flew in to Los Angeles to give support to my campaign. She was suffering so much that she could not stay more than a few days. She smiled bravely at the press cameras, made two short speeches, and shook hands with hundreds of people. I still don't understand how she managed to look healthy.

The odds against the American Independent Party getting on the ballot in all fifty states were almost insurmountable. It meant grueling work for thousands of supporters and large amounts of money from the "grass roots." It was definitely a movement of the people, as the contributions were in five-, ten-, and twenty-dollar bills.

I was still undecided about making a formal commitment to run, because Lurleen's health had me deeply worried. But she refused to let me say no. "Remember, George, you made a promise to the people of Alabama. We have been heckled, we have been stoned, we have tried to bring a message to the American people. What we have done and what we stand for is bigger than my life and yours. Please go on with the fight. I would never forgive myself if you quit because of me." It wasn't just her words, it was her earnestness that caused my throat to clog with emotion, and I had to wipe tears from my eyes.

I talked to the doctors about the problem. One said that Lurleen was really worried about the possibility of my allowing her illness to cause me to break a promise to the people of Alabama.

I still didn't want to commit myself. Just before Christmas, Lurleen's pains became so intense she could hardly move. Frightened by constant, throbbing pangs, she nevertheless refused to let them spoil her favorite season. She decorated the tree, shifting from side to side in an attempt to ease the pain. She wrapped family gifts, along with hundreds of gifts for the Methodist Children's Home in Selma.

A tradition at the Governor's Mansion is a Santa Claus for orphan children. Hiding her own agony, Lurleen tried to make it a happy occasion for all the young visitors. She wept openly when one young child said, "I wish I could stay here with you for Christmas."

Lurleen shopped for the whole family, conquering her pain by an exhibition of sheer grit. All during December she made plans to take Lee to Colorado to show her the mountains and snow. But she made only one trip in December—a return to Houston at the end of the month for more radiation treatments. The doctors found a pecan-size nodule that was pressing a nerve on Lurleen's right side, but they were confident it could be dissolved or reduced with betatron treatments.

We once more moved into a Houston apartment, and I stayed with Lurleen while she underwent more powerful radiation treatments. I practically never left the room, conducting all my business by phone.

It still depresses me just to recall those days. We sat together in the evening doing our best to comfort each other. There were times when I had to shift my gaze to avoid seeing her physical deterioration. Sometimes, out of the corner of my eye, I could see her take a deep breath and almost faint from pain. Powerless to help, watching her suffer was almost more than I could bear.

What do you say under such circumstances? "Are you all right, sugar?" And her smile and reply, "I'm fine, just fine," fooled neither of us.

American Independent Party supporters in Houston asked us to attend the opening of their campaign headquarters. I didn't think Lurleen was up to it, but she insisted on going with me. She dressed in a white woolen outfit and a mink stole, and more than six hundred enthusiastic supporters crowded into a five-room vacant house. They were all bent on cheering us up.

"You sure do look pretty, Governor."

"Fine—feeling just fine, thank you."

"We are praying for you, Governor."

"We're gonna vote for George Wallace when he runs for president. He's gonna show those folks, isn't he?"

How she kept smiling that night I shall never understand. She could hardly bear the pain, and after the speeches were over she rushed to our room to suffer alone.

On January 20 we made ballot position in California. I went to Washington, where I announced that I was in the race irrevocably. Lurleen telephoned me from Montgomery that she was happy and relieved that I had made it official. She had confided to Catherine Steinecker, "I hope I can make it until after November."

She was scheduled to return to Houston in late February for more treatments. But on February 22 she was rushed to St. Margaret's Hospital for four hours of emergency surgery. It was an intestinal obstruction, and it meant removing a portion of her colon and a nodule that was pressing on a nerve.

For two months Lurleen alternately rallied and relapsed. Sometimes she managed to walk in her hospital room. When she started to eat solid foods, we made preparations to bring her home. Then a new complication developed: an abscess formed on the abdominal wall and could be treated only by surgery. This performed, she once more started to improve and our hopes for her recovery were buoyed.

Then came the pulmonary embolus and a gradual loss of strength. In spite of all our protests, she demanded to be taken home to celebrate Lee's seventh birthday—and she had her way.

It wasn't so much the long strain, but a sense of complete helplessness, that was getting to me. I tried to nourish a hope that she would live, and I started grasping at medical panaceas. Was there a chance the doctors had overlooked some new medicine in some foreign country? Would a miracle happen at the last moment?

I canceled political engagements to be with her. Then she would look at me and say, "George, there's something funny about you canceling that trip." Then I'd mumble something about being tired and not wanting to go. She had a morbid fear about my going to Dallas, and I managed to hide from her the fact that I had made a speech there.

I also begged out of going to Vietnam.

While I was governor I had bought a house that Lurleen had always wanted. She liked the mansion, but she wanted a home to call her own. Wan and in pain, she asked to be taken to see the house and sit in it for a little while. "I want a new living room and some new dining-room furniture for the house. This can be my Christmas present, birthday present, and anniversary present, all combined."

She became upset if any of us interrupted our normal activities on her account. "George," she ordered, "you just go down to the office. If you keep hanging around here, I'll think I'm worse off than I am." I pretended to leave, but usually just went downstairs and sat.

Lurleen talked about the children. "George, Lee is so young and so little. I hope she doesn't forget what her mother looked like. Don't let her forget me."

"Lurleen, you're going to be here a long time. Besides, Lee could never forget you—she looks so much like you."

Whenever I thought I was about to break down, I went to the bathroom to regain my composure. I didn't want Lurleen to know that I was losing hope in those last few weeks.

She never lost her faith. "George, I know there is an afterlife. If worst comes to worst, and we die—well, we never really die. People meet in heaven. We can meet in heaven."

I became more and more restless and could not sleep. On Monday, May 6, I knew she wouldn't make it through another day. The doctors gave her shots to ease the pain, but they didn't help much. They re-examined her to see if they had missed anything, but there was nothing that could be done to save her or to relieve the pain. Even while dying, Lurleen made a typically gracious gesture: she asked Mary Jo Ventress, a very dear friend of my family, to prepare coffee for the doctors.

In response to my anxious query, the doctors shook their heads. "We don't expect her to live through the night."

I went into the room and took Lurleen by the hand. "George," she said, "I'm in a lot of pain. You're going to have to help me. I want you to stay with me all night tonight." Then she looked up at the doctors. "Please stay with me—I'm going to need all of you tonight."

She squeezed my hand tightly in her thin hands and tears began to flow. Then she quickly composed herself and said, "I'm sorry." I heard her say a little prayer: "Oh, God, please let me live, because I want to live. But if I can't live, please help me face whatever I have to face."

I spoke gently to her. "Lurleen, honey, we are all with you. We all love you. Your mother and daddy are here and all of your children." I held back my tears. "Lurleen, I love you. If you hear me, sweetie, squeeze my hand."

Her hand tightened on mine.

I asked the doctor, "Muscular?"

"Voluntary," he replied.

I sat holding her hand, and slowly her grasp relaxed. Her breathing had stopped.

"Is she gone?" I asked.

The doctor nodded.

When everyone had left, I sat with her alone. Before I left, I kissed her and ran my hand through her hair.

Waiting downstairs was the attendant from the funeral home. "Please treat her gently," I requested.

It was estimated that thirty thousand people came to pay their respects to Lurleen when she lay in state. Many eyes were clouded with tears. There were young and old, black and white, tall and short, people from every station in life. Many were my political foes—but they were there, too.

The state and military ceremonies were solemn and impressive. Lurleen had asked that Handel's "Water Music" be played during the march from the mansion to the capitol. Behind the motorcade bearing the casket, the 151st Army Band marched in slow cadence.

Before leaving for Montgomery's Greenwood Cemetery, religious services were held in St. James Methodist Church. The Reverend Vickers conducted a short and simple service, carrying out Lurleen's prior instructions. She had asked him to read the following poem, by an unknown author:

I love you not only for what you are but for what I am when I
am with you.

I love you not only for what you have made of yourself
but for what you are making of me.

I love you for the part of me that you bring out.

I love you for putting your hand into my heaped-up heart and
passing over all the foolish, weak things that you can't
help dimly seeing there, and for drawing out into the light
all the beautiful belongings that no one else had looked quite
far enough to find.

I love you because you are helping me to make of the lumber
of my life not a tavern but a temple. Out of the works of my
every day not a reproach but a song.

The Reverend Vickers told the mourners: "This great lady of our state embraced the three essential qualities for greatness—those being sincerity, compassion, and humility."

I sat and listened in numbed grief. During the heartfelt tributes my thoughts wandered back to when I had first met Lurleen, in the dime store, and went back and told Glen Curlee I had met the girl I was going to marry. I remembered Glen going to see her and reporting back to me that I was robbing the cradle. I thought how we had married on less than a shoestring and how our short honeymoon had ended in separation. So many things came back to me: her nightly telephone calls from "Mom" Sanders' house to me at the Quachita College campus in Arkadelphia, how she had followed me from base to base, the time she caught the crowded train to go home to wait for Bobbie to be born. The long bombing runs over Japan, praying that I would make it home to her and our baby; the single room she had made into a home; her working for my first political victory when she was herself too young to vote. I reproached myself for all the things I should have done and didn't—and for numerous things I had done.

I looked up from the grave as five National Air Guard F-84 jets swooped down over the knoll in "V" formation. One of the four planes broke off from the formation and disappeared, leaving four planes, symbolic of the loss of a comrade.

That night, I slept in the house she loved but never got to live in.

NOT A DIME'S WORTH OF DIFFERENCE

> *"You can take all the Democratic candidates for President and all the Republican candidates for President. Put them in a sack and shake them up. Take the first one that falls out, grab him by the nape of the neck, and put him right back in the sack. Because there is not a dime's worth of difference in any of them."* [GCW]

Not long after Lurleen's death, I discovered a letter written by Lee to her mother. It read:

"Dear Mama. I love you. I didn't no [know] you were going to heaven so soon. I thought we were going . . ."

I asked Lee, "Honey, you didn't finish the letter to Mama. Where did you say you were going?"

Lee answered sadly, "Daddy, I thought we were going to the lake and fish. Mama said when she got well, we would go fishing."

We were lonely without Lurleen's love and warmth. The nights were worst of all for me. I sat for hours listening to her favorite music on records. I spent many other hours in the cemetery and was becoming morbid. Nothing seemed to help me forget her terrible agony.

Only the presence of my daughters and young George helped me through those anguished days and nights.

The presidential campaign began in earnest in the late summer of 1968. I was forced to become active politically. This helped me get away from myself. I plunged eagerly into the political battle as leader of the newly formed American Independent Party.

The party had been born in protest. Our middle class, ignored and neglected by the Democratic and Republican parties, now would be heard from and represented. We would offer them more than a dime's worth of difference in political choices.

Rising taxes and inflation were the scourge of the middle class, who carried on their backs the non-producers and welfare loafers. Helplessly, they had watched first the slow, then the rapid, erosion of their economic reserves. Ironically, the super-rich, by using tax shelters and their personal tax-free foundations, avoided most of the tax burden. The middle class, more than any other group, needed relief from tax inequities and the indifference of the two major parties.

My platform in 1968 was neither revolutionary nor extreme. It called for equity: curtailment of foreign aid to our enemies even if it meant loss of profit, reform of our welfare program to eliminate abuses, an end to the federal government's encroachment in areas belonging to the states, an end to busing of little children to achieve racial quotas, and an end to judicial usurpation.

Middle-class patriotism and industry had supported our country in peace and war. Middle-class stability and hard work had produced the social health of our nation. It was shocking to see hard-working Americans struggling to make ends meet while millions got by without working. Not unstrangely, the parasites attacked the very people whose resources they sucked.

Middle-class Americans work for simple goals, which only a distorted mentality can regard as sinful. What is wrong with a desire to accumulate savings for our children's education, to make home improvements, to provide for our old age?

Another social rodent was gnawing on middle-class resources: Crime had reached such proportions it could no longer be ignored. To stop the rising crime rate, most Americans felt it was time to punish the criminal and not abridge the constitutional rights of the law-abiding.

I believed then and believe now that the family is the best guarantee against social dissolution and corruption. Wherever there is strong family tradition and cohesion, society will be vigorous and healthy. Child-care centers run by the government are no substitute for the father-and-mother influence in the family. The discarded cliché of love of God, love of country, and love of family is still the basis of a sound society. Love of all God's creation is as important as education to save our fragmenting social order.

Problems created by Washington bureaucrats have helped to destroy our inner cities. Forced shuffling of pupils from one neighborhood to another has not produced racial harmony—and much less has it provided quality education. The flight of the middle class to the suburbs has deprived the cities of important tax support.

Pseudo intellectuals, applying unworkable theories to society's problems, have merely managed to compound them. Now the same people who expanded the problems ask our indulgence while they dig once more into Pandora's box for new solutions.

The American Independent Party's success at the polls in 1968 astounded professional politicians in both parties. But it was no surprise to me or my collaborators. In future elections this large segment of the electorate would have to be taken into account by party leaders; to fail to do so would be to court disaster at the polls.

When we started the third party, we had no organization and no established sources of funds. Our income came principally from the "little man" all over the nation. By his contributions, we raised the money to gain ballot position and to finance the campaign. We did not have purse power, but we did have people power.

Our campaign workers handed out petitions at rallies, asking for contributions. Often we would receive petitions with more than a hundred signatures, each signer contributing one dollar. We acknowledged every contribution when it was accompanied by a name and address.

We collected approximately seven million dollars, most of it in small contributions. I was proud of the work done by my staff and by thousands of loyal volunteers who helped to get us on the ballot in all fifty states. The cynical political pros told us it was an impossibility. The loyal amateurs proved them wrong.

Former Governor Marvin Griffin of Georgia graciously agreed to become the party's stand-in candidate for the vice-presidency until a formal choice could be made. He was an able man who would have made a strong candidate himself. But at that time we were trying to avoid having two candidates from the same section of the country. I'm not sure that really matters much any more. I believe people today are less concerned about the part of the country a candidate comes from and more interested in his views and programs. Marvin Griffin was more than a stand-in candidate; he was a great morale builder and adviser to me during the whole of the 1968 presidential campaign.

I was more than pleased with the choice the American Independent Party made for my running mate. General Curtis LeMay was a distinguished gentleman with an outstanding military and civilian record. His acceptance cost him an excellent job, but he was a man completely willing to face personal sacrifice and even business ostracism in order to defend his political ideals.

A highly intelligent person, his direct and honest approach was as refreshing as it was often disconcerting to his admirers, who occasionally winced when the General spoke his mind with absolute frankness, to the almost sadistic glee of hostile reporters long accustomed to official ambiguity. I still maintain the highest respect for General LeMay, and my only regret is that a man of his stature and forthrightness had to learn the hard way that candid answers to loaded questions are not always the best political strategy.

Writing a coherent and realistic political platform for the American Independent Party was no easy task. We were made up of diverse people with diverse views. All were strongly individualistic and anxious for their ideas to be incorporated in the platform. Some felt betrayed if their pet aspect of the conservative philosophy was left out of a speech or campaign literature. A very few regarded everyone in government as a Communist or Communist dupe. I felt strongly about avoiding extremist views that could only hurt the party's image. In the end we put together an intelligent and level-headed platform.

I deliberately left out the Federal Reserve System as a prime political issue, although I am convinced the central banking system needs more vigilance and control. But the subject was complex, and I knew that most Americans would turn off the TV if we spent our time hammering at the Federal Reserve System. We had to stick to bread-and-butter issues if we were to capture the attention of voters. Middle America was concerned about taxes, inflation, school busing, law and order, and wasteful spending.

Other sincere conservatives wanted me to attack the United Nations. Americans who had so long regarded the UN as a device for keeping the peace and building a better world were slowly waking up to the true nature of the world organization. But 1968 was not an opportune time to proclaim grim truths.

It's different today. Now more and more Americans are having second thoughts about the UN. They want to know why we are in an organization that is so consistently anti-American. They want to know why we subsidize nations who take from us but, in and outside the UN, attack us. I believe the role of the United States in this diplomatic tower of Babel needs some profound rethinking. Americans today are ready to evaluate U.S. participation in the UN from self-interest, not from fuzzy, do-gooder innocence.

After Curtis LeMay became my running mate, I began to campaign actively in every part of the United States. I was received by tremendous and enthusiastic crowds wherever we held rallies. The few hecklers we encountered were played up by the news media to distort the true picture. Hecklers were no more numerous at my rallies than they were in the Nixon or Humphrey crowds.

People who threw rocks, bottles, and other dangerous objects at my rallies were called "demonstrators." Those who did the same thing during Nixon or Humphrey rallies were correctly called hoodlums, thugs, and anarchists.

In Toledo, Ohio, I spoke to an overflow crowd of more than twenty thousand. In the front rows were perhaps twenty or thirty heckers, booing and screaming obscenities to drown out my speech. My supporters began to chant, "Out—throw the bums out!" I asked the crowd to ignore the noisemakers, but it got so bad the police had to take a hand. The demonstrators were provoked to more violence when the police read the act of "disturbing the peace." Chairs and bottles were thrown before the hecklers were finally ejected.

Sometimes in an audience of ten thousand or more supporters there would be twenty or thirty boobs yelling, "*Sieg Heil!*" and waving Viet Cong flags. In Minneapolis we encountered the most vicious anti-war militants—most of them imported from other states to do their thing. The mayor unwittingly played into their hands by ordering the police to use minimal force. Many of our volunteer workers were young girls who passed out petitions to help us get on the presidential ballot in Minnesota. Suddenly, while petitions were being signed, the agitators descended on the girls, tore the petitions from their hands, and even knocked a few of the girls to the floor. Tardily, the police moved in to restore order.

The next day, the mayor apologized to me, and I appreciated his obvious sincerity.

At the airport in Albuquerque, New Mexico, I told a crowd, "The war in Vietnam is unpopular with most Americans. I am not sure we should be there, but as long as our servicemen are there we must give them our full support to win the war. There are a few who want the Communists to win . . ." I didn't get a chance to continue. A young man in the audience yelled, "I want them to win!" Someone in the crowd knocked him down and he would have been soundly thumped if I had not intervened.

To this day I fail to understand the toleration for those who were giving "aid and comfort to the enemy." Tokyo Rose did no worse in World War II, but she was tried for treason.

I believe in dissent. It would be a pretty dismal society if we had to keep our contrary opinions to ourselves, as people in the Communist nations are forced to do. There were sincere dissenters in New England who opposed the Mexican War in 1847; Abraham Lincoln was strongly outspoken against that war. There were dissenters during the bloody Civil War; people in North and South alike thought that the war could have been settled through negotiation. Our two world wars have had sincere and intelligent dissenters, from Debs to Lindbergh. But dissent is one thing; working actively for the enemy is something very different.

There were light moments during the campaign. On one occasion I was flying over the southern end of the Sierra Nevada, accompanied by members of the press. Looking back, I realize I probably shouldn't have given in to an urge to be boyishly prankish—and perhaps take out a little of my spite against some of the media people who had been taking pot shots at me for so long.

Looking at the radarscope, I noticed a number of build-ups that indicated bad weather ahead. My pilot, Jimmy Baswell, suggested we fly between the thunderstorms, but I thought it would be more prudent to turn back to the nearest airport. The newsmen saw occasional flashes of lightning in the skies but were not too concerned. They knew I seldom chanced bad weather.

I got on the plane's mike and assumed a doomsday tone. "Ladies and gentlemen, the weather ahead looks bad. My pilot has asked permission to fly through to our destination, Los Angeles. He thinks we can make it. I am not so sure. I'm worried about you good fellows. Look out there. It's really bad. If we go ahead, this plane is going to get a real shaking. But if we don't make it, I'll have the consolation of knowing I have taken along with me a bunch of dudes that have misread my campaign from coast to coast.

"But out of consideration for you, I'm willing to put it to a vote. Majority rule is the name of the game."

I asked all in favor of flying on to raise their hands. I raised mine. I was the only one.

"All right; you fellows write tough, but you're chicken underneath."

I gave the pilot instructions to turn back to Las Vegas. As the plane banked and took a new course, none of the newspaper people were aware that Jimmy Baswell had already received previous orders from me to turn back.

On another occasion, after a long day of campaigning in Philadelphia I held a press conference in a downtown hotel. I needed sleep and rest, and hoped the conference would be short. The newsmen were kind to me and kept it brief. Just when I thought the last question had been asked, a young lady reporter from Sweden nailed me on the subject of atomic energy. Her questions were technical and more appropriate at a seminar of nuclear physicists. To escape her, I announced, "Miss, if I am elected president, my friend and confidant Dr. Glen Curlee will be my atomic-energy director. He will be happy to answer any of your questions."

Poor Glen, sage of Ellmore County, was trapped. In a smug and superior tone of voice the reporter asked, "Dr. Curlee, precisely what will be your atomic-energy program?"

Glen fidgeted and made a few grimaces before answering. "Why, Sugah, the only thing I kin tell the guv'nah at this time is that we's gonna sell the bombs after we've done juiced 'em up. Yes, ma'am, we kin make us some money for a change, and make them countries happy that ain't got the bomb."

Glen was starting to warm up to the situation. "I can say right now and here, we's goin' into the bomb-making business. Our slogan is MORE BOOM PER BOMB! By the way, Sugah, does yore country have a bomb?"

Shades of our law-student days! Everyone present was either dumfounded or laughing. The poor reporter wasn't prepared for spoofing and made a hasty retreat, leaving the entire news corps chuckling.

In real life today, Glen Curlee is an able district attorney in Wetumpka. He is wise in knowledge of the human heart and is one of the most kindly persons I have ever known. Unfortunately, Glen is one of the last of a dying breed of southern raconteurs. Politics would be much duller without Glen Curlee around to spice it.

With the exception of the Vietnam War, the issues in the 1976 campaign are remarkably like the ones in 1968. There are faces in Washington, but as I once heard an Alabama farmer say, "You can't purify the water in a well by painting the pump." Here are several of the issues that still remain, some of them more serious than ever before and all of them being systematically bungled by party pros.

Education and Freedom of Choice

People throughout the nation, including Alabama and the rest of the South, accept non-discrimination as essential in a public education system. The dual school systems that existed prior to the Supreme Court decision outlawing them were not considered discriminatory in the states where they existed. We felt that type of school system was in the best interests of both races.

It's all academic now, of course, because strictly legal issues have taken precedence over "best interests." The dual school system was declared unconstitutional, and the so-called policy of non-discrimination has become law by court order and legislative enactment.

Few people have any quarrel with the principle of non-discrimination, but more and more we are coming to realize that the way it was handled and is still being handled is a blunder, creating at least as many injustices as it set out to correct. I still oppose, and I believe the people of the entire nation oppose, the contrived school situations we have now in the United States. It makes no sense whatsoever to destroy neighborhood schools through the device of quotas and percentages, and the whole concept of cross-city busing is nothing short of insanity. I believe this busing system will be resisted wherever it exists as long as it exists. One thing that has made people so cynical about government is that so many national politicians have promised to oppose this idiocy but have lacked the guts to take a stand or take action.

There is, of course, a simple and obvious solution—so simple and so obvious that it has never occurred to any of the professional reformers.

The solution is freedom of choice.

We should allow any child or parent or guardian to choose any school in the school district. For example, in the city of Montgomery, we sent out cards to every parent or guardian of every child, white or black or any other color, listing all the schools for their children's age groups. The parents checked the school they wanted, and that was the school the child was assigned to. If the child lived on one side of town and wanted to go to school on another side of town, he could do so freely—no coercion, no threats, no force, regardless of what the media or anyone else said.

The following year, the Justice Department and those who had fought the dual system said this freedom-of-choice system was not working. The reason they gave: there were not enough children on one side of town going to school on the other side!

We argued that the parents should make the choice instead of the government or some addle-brained child-shuffler. But we lost. They destroyed the freedom-of-choice system in favor of arbitrary quotas and racial balances and asinine busing.

In Montgomery, the capital of Alabama, some half dozen different school orders have been issued in the past seven or eight years. The result has been absolute chaos for the children. A situation has been created in which a child goes to the ninth grade in one school, is uprooted and planted in the tenth grade in another school, then is dropped back to the ninth grade again in another reshuffling—never getting to stay in any one school long enough to learn his way to the bathroom.

The Justice Department did all this on the authority of court decisions based on the Fourteenth Amendment. One of the festering sores in this country is the fact that people are not permitted to choose on issues vitally affecting their own lives and destinies. The liberal philosophy, freely but accurately translated, is "Don't let our idiot citizenry decide anything for themselves." That's why we have had the degrading spectacle of a large metropolitan school system (Boston) being run by a federal judge.

Law and Order

I suppose psychologists and sociologists and criminologists and other "ists" can come up with a lot of different explanations for the increasing incidence of crime—especially violent crime—in America. I don't like to quarrel with specialists whose training should give them greater understanding of the problem than I have, but some of the so-called solutions that are propounded and put into effect leave me wondering about their common sense.

If poverty is really the prime breeding ground of crime, then Barbour County in my boyhood days should have had one of the highest crime rates in the nation. After learning of the shenanigans of people in high places and affluent conditions, I am convinced that basic honesty and respect for one's fellow man are independent of poverty or riches. I accept the economic and sociological fact that slum conditions and deprival offer greater temptations to petty and serious crime, but something the do-gooders never manage to explain satisfactorily is how one brother in a poor family grows up honest and law-abiding while another becomes a thief or a mugger. Somewhere along the line, individual character and temperament make a difference—a difference that all the best-intentioned investigation in the world is not likely to explain.

Just as the individual factor is often decisive in creating a criminal, it should be equally a factor in meting out punishment. Justice without mercy is not justice. But crime without effective punishment is merely an invitation to more crime. And in spite of the rash of TV series attempting to glorify the policeman and rescue him from the "pig" classification, the fact remains that legal loopholes and overindulgent court decisions have weighted the scales in favor of the criminal against an arresting officer. I have frequently made the quip that you can get mugged in the park in the morning and before you can get to the hospital the mugger is out on personal-recognizance bond and the arresting policeman is on trial before the police review board for twisting the mugger's arm while taking him to the station. I read some time ago of a Washington man who was arrested for rape for a fourth time—technicalities had protected him against going to trial for the first three. This sort of thing is not only demoralizing to the police force, it constitutes an active menace for law-abiding members of society.

Yet this is precisely the situation that bleeding hearts and judicial toleration have fomented, aided by the tidal wave of violence and sick sex portrayed in the movies and on television. I have sat in judgment, and I know what an awful and sobering thing it is to have power of life or death, liberty or confinement, over another human being. Anyone who troubles to examine my record will find that I tried to be understanding and lenient where I felt there were mitigating circumstances; but I was severe where I felt that the case merited severity. I learned that every case is different; you can't apply the same criterion to all of them. One thing that justice should seek, however, is to make punishment both swift and certain—to avoid the present situation, in which the most flagrantly guilty criminal, a potential danger to society, has an eight-to-one chance of getting off scot free and being turned loose with the absolute conviction that crime is really not too risky a business after all.

I have in mind the particular absurdity of giving so many concurrent sentences. This means that an armed hold-up man can assault you and take your money; he gets caught and is soon out on bond. And while he is out, he commits seven more assaults and is caught and convicted for all of them. He winds up getting concurrent sentences—which in effect means he committed the eight robberies for the price of one. If a criminal knew he might be put away for fifty years in the penitentiary, he would think twice before going out on new assault sprees. And a lot of innocent lives might be spared in the process.

I have regretfully come to the conclusion that capital punishment is necessary as a deterrent for particularly ugly murders. Here, again, much depends on the special circumstances and the individual involved. Perpetrators of fatal stabbings and shootings that are a consequence of deliberate assault and robbery deserve, in my view, the death penalty. So do those who kill for sheer terrorism. I can't imagine how anyone can have any sympathy for those who were responsible for that barbaric bombing at La Guardia Airport in which so many innocent people were killed or maimed.

When Alabama restored the death penalty last year, the media portrayed me as almost gleefully looking around for someone to hang. This is, of course, absurd. Any person who takes sadistic pleasure in capital punishment is unfit to be a judge, in fact unfit to occupy any public office. But, by the same token, any judge or other public official who places the interests of the criminal above those of the victim is equally derelict of his duty. In general, I agree that punishment should be meted out with the view of rehabilitation—and capital punishment certainly does not fit that concept. But there are cases in which the criminals are so depraved—or so fanatically politically motivated—that rehabilitation is impossible or unthinkable. Society's respect for their lives should be no greater than their respect for the lives of members of society. To put them to death, after full legal process, is not only a fitting punishment for their acts but a deterrent and warning to others who are tempted to follow their example.

I have no desire to see death rows filled. But I believe the death penalty—in isolated instances of calculated and vicious murder—is a necessary means of protecting the lives of the law-abiding members of society.

Defense and Foreign Policy

The United States must be supreme militarily if it is to conduct an effective and intelligent foreign policy. This means we must have a military capacity second to that of no other existing or potential enemy or combination of enemies. And by military capacity I refer to both manpower and arms—the latter being convention, nuclear, or others as yet undeveloped. The price of falling behind in military strength will be our liberties and our very existence as a nation.

I am skeptical of détente, for the very simple reason that I distrust Soviet leadership. There is nothing in Soviet statements or actions to lead us to believe that the Kremlin has abandoned or even modified its ambitions to communize the world by first "burying" the United States. A relaxation of tensions is all to the good as long as we are under no illusions about the duplicity of the Soviet Union's Communist leadership. They may talk friendship and trade and understanding, but their actions on the world scene belie their protestations of amity. At the very time when traditional colonial powers have been voluntarily divesting themselves of their foreign dependencies, the Soviet Union has been actively enveloping many of them in its web of Communist imperialism. Slowly and relentlessly, we have permitted ourselves to become encircled by emerging states and "independent" former colonies that in reality are puppets of Soviet policy and servants of Soviet goals.

I have growing misgivings about the United Nations as an instrument of world peace and harmony. During recent years it has proved to be a divisive influence, in which the bloc formed by tiny new nation-states has consistently displayed its irresponsibility and its anti-U.S. bias.

No one nation, including the United States, should dominate the United Nations. By the same token, neither should it be dominated by any bloc of nations. I doubt whether the United Nations, with its absurd "one nation, one vote" makeup, will ever again be anything but a chaotic tower of Babel in which everything the United States stands for will encounter overwhelming and bitter opposition.

It would be regrettable if U.S. public opinion—which is increasingly turning against continued U.S. participation in the United Nations—were to pull our nation out of this body. After all, the UN does carry out some very laudable humanitarian and social programs, financed in large part by the huge U.S. quota. I do not recommend a pull-out at this time, but if the current trend continues (as I fear it will) an outraged American citizenry will demand that we get out. At the very least, it will insist that some means be found to make it impossible for U.S. taxpayers' funds to be employed in programs and actions having no other purpose than to destroy the United States and its democratic friends and allies.

I view it as nothing short of collective suicide for the United States to be shelling out huge sums of taxpayers' money in economic aid to declared enemies and to nations whose vote in the

United Nations has been consistently anti-American and anti-democratic. I am outraged whenever any of these Soviet stooge countries express indignation at U.S. threats to withhold foreign aid to nations that vote anti-American in the UN. They call it blackmail, and they issue noble statements about accepting no conditions for their votes. This is a legitimate exercise of their sovereignty. But while their votes may not be conditional, U.S. economic aid can and should be. I favor a foreign-aid policy in which the United States is as tight-handed with its foes as it is generous with its friends.

I favor liberal U.S. assistance to developing countries to help them help themselves out of the economic doldrum's, with no other condition than that they show themselves to be, if not our friends, at least not actively our enemies.

The Panama Canal issue will undoubtedly have to be faced by the next administration. I sympathize with the legitimate desire of any nation or people to have full sovereignty over its territory and to participate fully in the operation and proceeds of a project of the magnitude and importance of the Panama Canal. I believe many of the terms of the original Panama Canal treaty were unfair and unreasonable, a consequence of negotiations based on the best interests of the bankrupt French company rather than the best interests of Panama. I believe some means can and should be found to phase out exclusive U.S. control over the Panama Canal and the Canal Zone over a period of, say, the next twenty-five years, at the same time arriving at a mutually satisfactory basis for the construction of a sea-level replacement.

I am unalterably opposed, however, to any immediate or short-term pull-out or giveaway. I further believe that no negotiations should be conducted and certainly no treaty concluded with the Soviet-oriented dictatorship that at present controls Panama. We have only one alternative—to stand fast with the existing treaty, with the sincere promise that we will negotiate in good faith and understanding a new treaty with a lawfully elected democratic regime in Panama.

Judicial Encroachment

I believe the Constitution as devised by our founding fathers was intended to keep the federal government—and especially the federal judiciary—from meddling in internal affairs of the states. If the sense of the people has changed since those days, then the proper way to permit what the Constitution specifically prohibits is to adopt a constitutional amendment eliminating the Tenth Amendment, which reads: "The powers not delegated to the United States by the Constitution, nor prohibited by it to the States, are reserved to the States respectively, or to the people."

I see this issue as fundamental and vital. I deplore the situation in which a few sinecured men on the Supreme Court decide that the Constitution means something it clearly does not mean. An unchecked federal judiciary is reaching into areas where it has no constitutional right to exercise authority.

It is not a question of whether this or that reform is desirable or not. Even the most desirable reforms can and should be brought about by strictly legal means, not as an end justifying the means.

There have been multiplying incidents of government by judicial edict. A federal judge makes a finding that overturns all prior precedent and is at complete odds with our Constitution. If anyone disobeys that order, the same judge cites that person for contempt and jails him without a jury trial. The irony of this is that federal courts have held that a newspaperman must reveal his sources of information, and when a reporter goes to jail defending his right to privileged information his colleagues refer to him as a martyr; but those same news media called it anarchy when they thought some people in the South were going to violate a federal court order.

The year 1976 being our bicentennial year, perhaps one of the points of emphasis should be how this precise process of government by judicial fiat triggered the American Revolution. The British Crown did not trust colonists on juries and resorted to harsh and arbitrary contempt citations against them; offenders were judged and jailed without trial. The judge was supreme then, and he is becoming equally powerful today. But what he is doing today is just as intolerable to modern-day Americans as the behavior of the Crown judges was to outraged colonists.

The judicial branch can today strike down anything the legislative or executive branch does, by the simple device of calling it unconstitutional. And the people have the choice of obeying, or defying and accepting the consequences. I do not advocate disobeying court orders. But I am increasingly alarmed by the expansion of judicial power into new areas and the arbitrary manner in which judicial orders are issued and enforced. Thomas Jefferson saw this coming. He once predicted that the judiciary would get around to stealing a little bit of authority here and a little more authority there, until a court-centered dictatorship resulted.

I am less worried about the power of the legislative or executive branches than I am about the unbridled voracity of the unelected judiciary. There is nothing to restrain them, no force or power that can override them. This is evident in the deep involvement of the federal judiciary in purely local issues involving state jury systems, state voting systems, state school systems, state penal systems. In one instance, a federal judge decided that a fully qualified expert at an Alabama mental hospital had violated a court order that set up rules and regulations for the treatment of mental patients. Judges today hand down complex "guidelines" having all the force of law on subjects for which they have no qualifications and certainly no constitutional authority.

In 1976 a federal judge decided he knew more about running the Boston school system than the elected school board. In effect, he decided that Boston voters have no right to run their schools the way they want to run them. It is immaterial here whether the voters or the school board are right or wrong; the point is that no federal judge should be allowed to set himself up as the unappealable authority.

I cannot accept the competence of the federal judiciary to determine policies involving the public schools (or other institutions) of any state or municipality. As long as it stands, the Tenth Amendment is a valid constitutional barrier to such action.

The executive and legislative branches of government are under the restraint imposed by the electorate. A few men appointed for life to our courts are under no such restraint. When legislators or presidents abuse their power or authority, the people can go to the polls and vote them out. They can force—and have forced—a President and a Vice-President out of office. Impeachment may be initiated against a member of the judiciary, but only on moral grounds, never because of abuse of authority.

The answer, of course, is to make the judiciary accountable to the people. Let them run for office and hold office for a stipulated period of time. Give them adequate compensation to provide incentive for good men to get involved in a political campaign. Then if the people get abusive judges, they have no one to blame but themselves—but they have a remedy at their disposal. I am not sure what would be a better way of selecting Supreme Court justices—and even if we found a better way, there is always the probability that the Supreme Court would find the new method unconstitutional. It's that powerful.

This relates directly to the whole issue of states' rights versus federal authority. We must never forget that the federal legislative and executive and judicial branches were created by the states, and that the creature cannot be superior to the creator. That such a thing could happen was one of the underlying fears of the founding fathers. That is why so many states refused to ratify the Constitution until the first ten amendments, or "Bill of Rights," were added.

Americans, North and South, who believe in the supremacy of the states over local issues and institutions have been maligned and will continue to be maligned as racists. This is unjust and false. Let the constitutional issues be resolved in the manner that the Constitution itself provides, and we will abide by the result, whether we agree with its principles or not.

These issues are just as pressing now as they were in 1968. I offer the foregoing comments as part of my political credo for today.

DESIGN FOR DEFEAT

A revolution does not march in a straight line. It wanders where it can, retreats before superior forces, advances wherever it has room, attacks whenever the enemy retreats or bluffs and, above all, is possessed of enormous patience. —Mao Tse-tung: Richard Hughes, New York Times Magazine, *Sept. 21, 1958.*

Thus we may know that there are five essentials for victory: (1) *He will win who knows when to fight and when not to fight.* (2) *He will win who knows how to handle both superior and inferior forces.* (3) *He will win whose army is animated by the same spirit throughout all the ranks.* (4) *He will win who, prepared himself, waits to take the enemy unprepared.* (5) *He will win who has military capacity and is not interfered with by his sovereign. Victory lies in the knowledge of these five points. —Sun Tzu Wu,* Art of War, *translated by Lionel Giles, Luzac & Co., London, 1910.*

The enigmas of the ill-fated U.S. involvement in Vietnam continued to puzzle me long after the 1968 presidential election. I wanted to go to Southeast Asia to obtain firsthand the information that would perhaps help explain our engagement with an enemy ten thousand miles from our mainland.

Since 1945, U.S. foreign policy had stumbled from one geopolitical blunder to another. Our efforts to contain communism had obviously failed. Following World War II, communism controlled Eastern Europe, with paper promises to allow free elections; China was conquered by communism with arms supplied from Russia; and in areas once controlled by European countries, communism rushed to fill the vacuum left by departing colonialists.

The perimeter of western democracy continued to shrink, while the Communist empires expanded.

Food, technology, and even weapons were exchanged for paper détente with our admitted foes. Lenin had cynically but truthfully predicted. "They will sell us the rope to hang them."

We had been told by our government that Southeast Asia was of strategic importance in the containment of communism. Then, why had we fought this war with our military's hands tied, why had our "allies" traded with North Vietnam, and why had we persisted in sending our young men to die in a no-win war?

Another important reason for going to Vietnam was to let our servicemen know that not all U.S. politicians were defeat-oriented. To me it was incomprehensible that while our young men were fighting a dedicated foe, a noisy minority at home was asking for a Viet Cong victory. To oppose the war was dissent—to advocate victory for the enemy was treason.

Recently President Ford suggested we pass over the Vietnam episode and move on with the agenda of running America. But can we afford to forget these blunders until we are sure we will not make more of them? The loss of fifty-five thousand men, nearly a half-million wounded, and 150 billion dollars down the drain requires an assessment of our foreign policy. U.S. survival rests on the correct interpretation of our past mistakes.

My journey of a month began in late October 1969.

After a short press conference at Saigon's crowded airport, we went directly to the Hotel Caravelle to spend the night. The next morning, we were escorted by Majors Huntsberry and Ring to Military Assistance Command Headquarters, where we had a very informative conversation with Major General Townsend. He briefed us on military operations in Vietnam and arranged for a field trip to "Black Virgin Mountain" the following day. That afternoon, we visited the 24th Evacuation Hospital at Long Binh. We had lunch with Brigadier General Bowers; his second in command, Colonel McClure; and his dedicated medical staff. I talked to the men in the wards and took the names of those from Alabama. The wounded were awaiting evacuation to the United States.

The following morning, we boarded a helicopter and flew to Black Virgin Mountain, known in Vietnamese as Mui Ba Den. This communications center on top of the highest mountain in this area of South Vietnam was garrisoned by men from the 25th Infantry Division.

A Major Dutcher told us that our troops controlled the top of the mountain, while the Viet Cong held the lower slopes and South Vietnamese were encamped at the mountain's base. He told us that the Viet Cong often broke through the barbed-wire barriers and destroyed equipment before being driven off. On occasion, the Viet Cong fired on landing and departing helicopters. These fire-support bases were scattered throughout enemy-held territory.

A fire-support base is a protected area separated from other military bases. It consists usually of an artillery battery guarded by a company of infantry. Day and night, our infantry ventured from their aerie to seek out the Viet Cong. These searching sweeps were part of defensive war tactics.

The officers, non-commissioned officers, and men were a fine, well-trained group. The following June, this fire-support base figured prominently in a North Vietnamese offensive. An attacking group that sought to overrun this garrison was repelled, with five hundred enemy losses.

We visited "Wood" fire-support base and found the same high morale and excellent training. It was thrilling to be so well received by the troops and to find them so little affected by their long absence from home. General Hollis, commander of the 25th Division, told us, "This kind of visit helps our morale. The men feel they are not forgotten."

The troops in Vietnam gave me a warm reception. There was much handshaking and photo-taking during our tours of the military camps. I derived much satisfaction in knowing that I had received more votes from the servicemen in Vietnam in 1968 than had the other presidential candidates.

Many of the South Vietnamese officials who escorted me were on the Communist death list if they lost the war. Those who cooperated with the Americans would be the first to be shot.

We talk about and hear a lot about détente. Détente means the relaxation of tension. Is this possible without military superiority of the United States? Is it possible when the Communist world continues its economic, political, and military expansion? Pretty words cannot conceal their lust for power.

The Viet Cong were told by their political commissars that the

United States has replaced French colonialism. "You must drive these foreigners out of your land."

During my talks with Malaysian leaders, I was frequently told that the United States should win the war militarily in Vietnam and stop worrying about China. They added, "If you are timid about China, then you should never have become involved in an Asian war."

Southeast Asian leaders knew we could not win against the North Vietnamese by fighting the war in South Vietnam. Many of them told me the United States should carry the war to Hanoi. But the rail lines bringing supplies from China were never bombed. Haiphong Harbor was a protected sanctuary for ships bringing supplies to the North Vietnamese. Why did we fight a terrible war with such self-imposed military handicaps?

We should not have entered this land war in Asia if we could not fight to win or if we lacked the national will to win. Sun Tzu Wu's book on the art of war states, "He will win who knows when to fight and when not to fight." Obviously, our politicians failed to understand this ancient oriental maxim of war.

Mr. Boozer of the U. S. State Department met us after our return from the field. He drove us to a lovely Saigon restaurant for dinner. While we were dining, the band played "Dixie," prompting me to ask the maître d'hôtel the name of the song. He replied, "I don't know, but the song means 'I like Alabama.'"

The dinner was delightful, but my thoughts while eating kept going back to the men at the fire-support bases and the "no-win" war they were forced to fight.

The next day, we were briefed at the embassy on aid to South Vietnam and the political prospects for the country. The conversations I had with Ambassador Bunker were frank and informative.

We visited navy units along the Mekong Delta. Conversation with navy officers increased my knowledge of the total military picture. The help we got from military, State Department, and civilian employees was of immeasurable value during our week and a half in South Vietnam.

The press did its best to accompany me to the field and to cover all my activities in South Vietnam. I had not come for publicity, and did not hunt it. The State Department had evidently received orders from Washington to play down my visit. Embassy sources would tell the newsmen that I was going to leave at 8 A.M. Then, late at night I would receive a call changing the departing time to 7 A.M. The newsmen showed up at eight only to find me gone. Sometimes they deliberately arrived early just to make sure they didn't miss me.

I had been invited to South Vietnam by President Thieu, with whom I had been scheduled to meet. But Washington decided against it. I fail to comprehend why the Washington crowd was so worried about my meeting with President Thieu. I had lost the election in 1968 and I had come for information, not political publicity. The day I was to confer with President Thieu, we were informed he could not see us. We were later told by a now retired State Department official that he had received orders from Washington to cancel our scheduled meeting.

Flying westward toward Bangkok, Thailand, I could look down on hundreds of square miles of jungle. The impact of this green vastness fortified my conviction that America could not police the world. If the governments of Southeast Asia could not rally their people against communism, then certainly foreigners could not.

When we landed in Bangkok we were met by Thai and U. S. Government representatives. I had a delightful lunch with Thailand's foreign minister, His Excellency Thanat. A learned and intelligent man, he told me he had a strong dislike for the New York *Times*. We made bets with each other on which of us had gotten the worst coverage from the *Times*. When I was leaving, he said, "Dear friend, we have much in common. We have both had our share of journalistic indecencies. I understand the problem for you in getting over to the people what you really believe."

The meal was my first experience with Thai cooking, and it was superb. After lunch I was driven to SEATO headquarters to meet with General Vargas, of the Philippines, who then presided over the defense organization. He had fought with the Americans against the Japanese in World War II. He had survived the Bataan Death March after the surrender of Corregidor by joint U.S. and Philippine forces. Later, he fought against the Huks, a Communist guerrilla organization that attempted to subvert the Philippines after World War II. General Vargas was very knowledgeable about the complex problems of Southeast Asia.

The Thai are a handsome and intelligent people who at that time had high respect for the United States. I do not know about their current views, after the military debacle in Vietnam.

During one of my few quiet moments in Thailand, I tried to organize my thoughts about my journey. I tried to prepare myself for an imaginary appearance on the U.S. television show "Meet the Press." I came to the conclusion the only thing I could say would be, "I don't know enough yet to say anything"—just the sort of public comment a trained politician should never make.

In Singapore, I met with the British high commissioner, Sir Arthur Delamar. He expressed his views about U.S. presence in Vietnam and British rule in Singapore. I was not surprised to learn the British planned to withdraw from this part of the world within two years. The British had the good sense to know when it was time to leave. This is political maturity.

One regret while in Singapore was that I did not have time to go to the Raffles Hotel, which was celebrating its 150th anniversary. Rudyard Kipling and other writers had written about this famous meeting place at the crossroads of the Orient.

Malaysia had successfully come from the brink of destruction in its war against Communist guerrillas ten years before. Now its economy boomed and its government appeared stable.

My visit to Taiwan was informative and enjoyable. The meals served at state dinners on this tight little island were the finest I had ever eaten. My meeting with Chiang Kai-shek lasted an hour. In the presence of this remarkable man I felt the futility of his dream of returning to the Chinese mainland. He seemed to be living in the backwash of history. But, then, some of history's greatest men have been on the losing side.

Throughout our stay in Taiwan I met friendly and intelligent people anxious to help and inform us. Before leaving, I had the pleasure of talking with Dr. Ku, former Secretary General of the World Anti-Communist League. I also enjoyed conversing with Professor Hsu, an authority on mainland history and a military analyst of great knowledge.

We were completely unprepared for snow when we landed at the airport in Seoul, Korea. All of us were still dressed for the tropics. Fortunately, the U. S. Embassy and Korean representatives rushed us to a warm VIP lounge, where I had a late-evening press conference before going to our hotel in downtown Seoul.

The next morning, I was driven to the residence of the U.S. ambassador, Mr. Porter, in my judgment the best-informed and most interesting person I met during the whole trip. He knew the language, culture, and history of Korea. I benefited by his knowledge of the Orient and appreciated his briefings before meeting with top Korean leaders.

President Park received us with magnificent hospitality. Members of the Korean cabinet toasted the United States and expressed their gratitude for U.S. help in preserving Korean freedom. "If America calls, we will send a hundred thousand troops," said President Park. Then, perhaps with a little embellishment, he added, "We will send you the number of troops you ask for."

Korea can resist communism, because it has military strength and the will to resist. Its troops in Vietnam were known to be fearless fighters.

My trip to the DMZ at Pan Mun Jom was an exciting experience. Eyeball-to-eyeball surveillance of each side's military moves keeps both on the alert. It was here I grasped the military motto the Communists understand best: strength!

I have no doubt the North Koreans would attack if it were not for South Korea's preparedness and its military alliance with the United States.

After an inspection of U.S. and South Korean troops, I sat down to a delicious meal of fried chicken—South Korean style—as good as any in Barbour County.

Flying home after more than a month in the Orient, I had an opportunity to reflect on all I had seen and learned. I had formed some short-term conclusions about South Vietnam. The South Vietnamese believed that in time they could take over the full burden of the military operations in South Vietnam. But, for the present and immediate future, they would need American fire support, airlifts, and tactical and strategic air support. They could not then go it alone.

The South Vietnamese military confessed that, while they were capable of containing small guerrilla units, large-scale military operations were not in their calculations. They were thinking in terms of a very long period of U.S. support and help. I got the impression from my talks with U.S. leaders that our plans were for South Vietnam to go it alone as soon as possible.

Americans lack the patience for a long war, and the North Vietnamese knew this. Unfortunately, our paper plans did not take into consideration either the oriental mind or the strength of the Communist will to hold out for victory no matter how long it was in coming.

Cleverly, after twenty years of guerrilla warfare, the North Vietnamese switched to more-conventional tactics. During the last months of the war in South Vietnam, the North Vietnamese Army swept south using massed tanks and infantry. In 1969 I had discussed with the South Vietnamese military their general strategy. They indicated they were not prepared for any radical change in their enemy's small-unit warfare.

After my return to the United States, my concern for our servicemen remained uppermost in my mind. Those left behind would fight and some would die in a lost cause. In America some of our citizens would continue to protest the war. The radical left would carry the Viet Cong flag and publicly advocate a Viet Cong victory. This group of traitors stayed out of jail on a legal technicality: Congress had not declared war.

The mass media had flattered and dignified these disgraceful clods with sympathetic prime-time coverage. There is an ancient oriental saying, "If I reward treason with good, how then shall I reward loyalty?"

Good men had gone to Vietnam believing that their service and sacrifice were needed. If they died in vain, the fault lay with their government, and not with them.

NEW START

With Lurleen's death, the governorship of Alabama went to her lieutenant governor, Albert Brewer. He was a former speaker of the Alabama House, having been elected in my administration. By custom, the governor's choice of speaker candidates is elected by the House membership.

He had run for the office of lieutenant governor as a loyal supporter of Lurleen, and he shared her overwhelming victory. During his term it became evident that a substantial part of his support was coming from my political opponents—from such people as Postmaster General Winston Blount, who stated publicly that Brewer was the best governor that Alabama had ever had during his lifetime.

This didn't bother me too much at the time, because, in 1970, I didn't really intend to run for governor again. I wanted to concentrate my efforts on the 1972 presidential campaign. Naturally I realized it would be to my advantage to have someone in the governorship who was sympathetic to me and my programs, someone who could give support to my national campaign. I was still hopeful that Brewer would remember that he had become governor largely as a result of my backing. His designation as vice-chairman of the Southern Governors' Conference was part of a movement by southern governors to strengthen my hand in case I became a presidential candidate.

It didn't work out quite that way. Many of the large newspapers that had been critical of me for years gave Brewer their backing, as did many other people in Alabama who had long opposed me. Somehow Brewer had received the impression that I was not going to run for governor under any circumstances. I went to the Governor's Mansion one night and talked with him to correct that impression. I told him I hoped he would not join those who had always worked so hard to keep me out of office—referring to the Democratic Party's national leadership in Alabama, the Republican Party, and many of the special-interest groups.

"If you run," commented Brewer, "you will win."

"Not necessarily," I told him. "That's up to the people of Alabama. No one is a sure winner. I don't know at this time whether I will run or not. But I do want you to know that I have never made any commitments not to run."

One by one, just about all the anti-Wallace elements became supporters of Brewer. Many who had reluctantly resigned themselves to Lurleen's victory in 1966 became gleefully active once more in backing the incumbent. It came as no surprise when the early polls showed him in the lead, although my own private soundings indicated that this was in large measure because people still regarded him as being pro-Wallace.

I played into Brewer's and my enemies' hands by announcing late. By that time, city and county officials who had any dealings with the state government had pledged themselves to Brewer. His campaign was well financed, giving credence to then unverified reports that money was coming not only from normal, Democratic sources but from Republicans as well. It wasn't so much that they were in favor of Brewer, but against me—hoping by electing Brewer to remove the base from which I could become a viable presidential candidate in 1972.

It wasn't until the Watergate investigations that the source of Brewer's campaign financing was finally revealed. Although a Democrat, he had received some four hundred thousand dollars from the Committee to Re-Elect the President. The Watergate gang was just as interested in stopping Wallace as it was in electing Republicans.

Brewer led in the first primary, as I had predicted to my supporters. "Tomorrow," I had told them, "I'm going to run second, and Charles Woods is going to run third." In the second primary, most of Woods's supporters came over to me, and I managed to win the second primary by a little more than thirty-five thousand votes.

In the general elections it was another story. With two or three opponents, I received what is probably the largest vote that any

Alabama governor ever obtained: 639,000. My recollection is that I carried every county.

Brewer later said that it had been a dirty campaign—and I agree with him. But most of the dirt was directed at me. I did my best to campaign strictly on the issues, leaving personalities to one side. I even praised Brewer as a fine gentlemen and said it was for the voters to decide. It was sincere praise, because I respected—and still respect—him and his fine family. Any reflections on him or his family on the part of any of my supporters during the campaign were done without my knowledge and certainly without my consent. And I want to give Brewer the full benefit of the doubt with respect to reflections on my family made by his supporters.

I really don't think these things matter too much with the voters. People don't like that kind of campaigning. Much of the dirt aimed at me had an out-of-state origin—scurrilous reports by national columnists, propaganda from both party headquarters in Washington, Internal Revenue Service investigations right in the middle of the campaign. I don't know where the money came from to finance the "helicopter incident": A chopper carrying people from the governor's office and the state photographer was flying over my brother Gerald's farm and force-landed in a pasture. There were no casualties and everybody ran away. What they were trying to accomplish is anyone's guess. Gerald commented, "If they wanted to come out and see my farm, they could have asked me and I would have extended an invitation."

The voters paid no more attention to the low blows than I did. They elected me to a second term. I regret very much that my victory alienated Albert Brewer, who has never to this day offered congratulations. His bitterness was evident on election night. I don't recall receiving any message from him when I was shot, although I would be unfair to state flatly that he didn't send one; millions of messages came, and I couldn't possibly see them all. I haven't seen Brewer personally since then, and it appears that he has deliberately avoided me. I remember being the speaker at a Masonic lodge at which he was the Grand Lodge office; he made it a point to leave before I arrived.

I'm genuinely sorry about this. After all, I recognized his merits in the early days of his political career; I wouldn't have appointed him speaker of the House if I hadn't had respect for him and confidence in him. True, every man has to go his own way, and Albert Brewer was and is a free man, as he demonstrated. I dislike losing supporters, of course. But losing friends hurts much more deeply.

The election over, I was set upon by a tiny but powerful pressure group consisting of my youngest child, Lee. Less than two months after Lurleen's death, young Lee came and sat beside me on the big master bed (sometimes she sneaked in to sleep with me).

"Daddy, when are you going to get married?"

"Honey," I replied, "I don't know about getting married. Why do you want me to get married?"

"Because I want a mother."

As the months passed, I realized that Lee needed and wanted a mother's touch and presence. After her mother died, Lee used to love to visit with Lurleen's friends and go places with them. And while I was slow in admitting it, even to myself, I needed a woman's touch and presence as much as Lee did.

So the one-child pressure group was merely pushing me in a direction I was was more than willing to move in. Shortly after the July 1970 elections, we were invited to stay at an island near Key West. I went with Lee, my older daughter Bobbie Jo and her husband, their infant and a friend of theirs, and my daughter Peggy Sue and a friend of hers. I remember commenting to Lee before we left, "What about asking Cornelia?"

I had seen Cornelia Snively during the primaries. Lee was delighted, because she knew that Cornelia liked swimming and fishing and hiking.

Cornelia did go with us, and I found myself resenting the fact that Lee monopolized just about all her time. Cornelia was nineteen years younger than I. I had previously thought of her only as a little girl I had known back in 1954, when I was involved in the Folsom campaign and she was a high school senior.

Cornelia had since grown into a witty, intelligent, pretty, and outgoing woman. She had married and raised a family of her own. Her mother, Ruby, is Big Jim's sister—and I am sure no one in either the Folsom or Wallace family ever dreamed that there would one day be a matrimonial link between them.

I recall a day in 1970 when Governor Folsom was opposing

my candidacy. He held a press conference at the home of Cornelia's mother. Cornelia was standing behind his chair when he said, "I want to tell you something about Wallace. He is a warmonger."

I asked Cornelia about this, and she gave me the none-too-flattering explanation: "Of all the things he wanted to call you, that was the least harmful to you. I really didn't want him to be overcritical, and I didn't object to that because it was probably the least unkind of the things he wanted to say about you."

Little by little I managed to ease Lee out of the picture and establish close relations with Cornelia. We were married in January 1971, with members of only the immediate families present. We spent our honeymoon in Florida (over Cornelia's objections, I invited some of my Alabama friends) and returned to Montgomery just before the inauguration on January 24.

Cornelia's ebullient presence has been an inspiration to me. A natural athlete, she inspires admiration as a water skier, swimmer, and boatswoman. Strikingly attractive, she has a strong mind; fortunately for me, where her views touch on politics they coincide with my own. And in areas in which we are not completely in agreement, we usually write off the subject by saying, "Oh, you Wallaces!" or "That's the Folsom in you!"

Big Jim has visited us on many occasions since our marriage, as he is very fond of Cornelia. Just as Cornelia has done an enviable job of rearing her own children, she has been a wonderful influence in my own family, under circumstances that must certainly have been trying and disheartening. The only complaint she has made about our demanding political activity is that it doesn't let us spend enough time with the children. It's a valid objection, but as a reality of politics the situation has no solution.

There is no question in my mind that Cornelia's presence has made Lee's childhood happy and well adjusted, which it probably would not have been otherwise. Her faith in my eventual recovery from that tragic episode in Laurel has been decisive in shoring up my own faith and determination.

Marriage to Cornelia expanded my family all at once, and I am just old-fashioned enough to cherish strong family ties. The oldest of my own children is Bobbie Jo, who was born when I was in the armed services. She graduated from the University of Alabama, married, and has two children.

The next, Peggy Sue, after graduating from Troy State University, adopted a wonderfully rewarding career—that of teaching exceptional, or "atypical," children. I have been very lucky with sons-in-law, as Bobbie Jo's husband, Jim Parsons, and Peggy Sue's, Mark Kennedy, are as talented as they are personable.

Our thirteen-year-old Lee, is active and sweet. She loves music and excels with the organ and piano—engaging in baton twirling as well. George, Jr., is now in his mid-twenties. His is a sensitive temperament. The loss of his mother when he was sixteen was a traumatic experience. He traveled with me during the 1968 campaign, performing on the guitar, singing, and making talks. After I was shot he dropped out of school to be close to me. He now attends Huntington College in Montgomery. His mature and thoughtful nature has helped me to understand—if not always to agree with—the thinking and outlook of the younger generation of Americans.

Cornelia's two children are Jim and Josh Snively, eleven and twelve years old, respectively. They are strong, healthy youngsters who play football and basketball—an interest in sports hardly surprising in children of such an accomplished athlete as Cornelia.

My brother Gerald has a successful law practice in Montgomery, and he owns a farm and several businesses, although it would be stretching things considerably to describe him as rich. He used to help me run my state election campaigns, and I still value his advice. I have no personal share in his business enterprises.

Gerald was adventurous and impatient as a boy, quitting high school to take a sixty-dollar-a-month job with the State Highway Department (a mammoth salary for a youngster in those days). He served with the Seabees in the South Pacific, and after discharge contracted tuberculosis, which meant long stays in VA hospitals. He finally had to have a lung lobe removed, and for a long time there was doubt about his recovery.

He entered law school at the University of Alabama on the GI Bill, graduating in 1959 and glossing over his grades by quoting the old law-school saying "A-students become professors, B-students become judges, and C-students make the money." Pointedly, politicians are not mentioned.

The youngest Wallace brother, Jack, is a circuit judge in Clayton—his penalty, no doubt, for having made better grades than either of his brothers. Jack and I practiced law together for several years, and as a judge he has gained a deserved reputation for fairness and humaneness. There is no doubt in my mind that he is the best lawyer in the family.

With my inauguration and the meeting of the legislature, I was deeply involved not only in Alabama affairs but in national politics once more. After my third-party campaign in 1968, people were asking whether Wallace was still a Democrat—and I had to ask and answer the same question for myself.

Although our third party had done amazingly well in the previous presidential campaign, I was convinced that we had achieved our purpose and that general support for a third party was waning. After all, the majority of the people of the nation were registered as Democrats. I had participated in the campaign for the state governorship as a Democrat, and I was convinced that my best role would be to work within the Democratic Party framework and provide a strong counterbalance against the so-called "liberal" wing. Incidentally, I could never understand why the fine word "liberal" should be applied to politicians who favor concentration of power in a central government, increasing interference with individual initiative, and reduction of the areas of states' rights. These things are the antithesis of true liberalism.

I believe the American people are aware of this anomaly and are increasingly incensed at repeated interference in state and local affairs, the scandalous excesses of the welfare programs, and the camel's head of bureaucracy that has insinuated itself into every aspect of our lives.

There was no question in my mind then, nor is there now, about my being a Democrat, although there was and probably still is a strong element in the party that would prefer to write me out. I remember the party hierarchy stating that they would accept anybody on the ticket but me. The trouble is that the Democratic Party has accepted and nominated candidates who pleased the hierarchy but were completely out of phase with the currents of sentiment and feeling of the vast majority of Democrats.

During 1970 and 1971 there was a great clamor by the press, headed by the New York *Times*, about the need to get the people involved in the election process and especially in the primaries. We don't hear much about that today, and the Raleigh *News and Observer,* which was so insistent about primaries being the right of the people, is now saying that the state primary law in North Carolina should be repealed, because it is cumbersome and doesn't attract the "leading" candidates. The problem could well be that the "leading" candidates too often don't attract much following.

I took on some of those leading candidates in 1972 and showed just how shallow their support really was. It started in Florida, where I had my first test of whether I could qualify as a Democrat. I had decided to skip the New Hampshire primary and concentrate on a state whose population is made up of people who have come from just about all the rest of the United States. Immigration to Florida has made the state quite cosmopolitan and not at all representative of its southern neighbors. I wanted to make my first attempt in Florida because I felt it was a good cross section of national viewpoints, although of course there is still a strong element of native Floridians who do identify themselves with the Deep South.

Once I obtained certification in Florida, I went in campaigning with all my strength. It was an encouraging reception, as I drew massive crowds all the way from Jacksonville to Miami and below. I found considerable similarity of viewpoint throughout the state, as people from Dade County to the Florida panhandle were concerned about the same issues.

There were eight or nine candidates in the primary race, although not all were "leading." In spite of pooh-poohing by the press, which tried to convince the people that there was no point in voting for me inasmuch as I could not possibly carry any state outside of the Deep South, I managed to outpoll them all. I received 42 per cent of the primary votes, and under the party's own rules I obtained seventy-five of the eighty-one delegates.

This unexpected backing in Florida convinced me that I was on the right track—that I was touching chords that appealed not only to Southerners but to the entire nation. I made a mistake, however, by not bouncing immediately out of my Florida victory into the Wisconsin primaries. Fact was, I didn't expect to do too well in Wisconsin, as the polls showed me running almost last. I dallied, toying with the idea of skipping Wisconsin and making a heavy play for some other state, where my chances might look better.

Somewhat belatedly, I decided to take my campaign into Wisconsin, although there was considerable apprehension that a poor showing would do irreparable damage to my nationwide campaign. We had no organization there, although the precedent existed of my 34 per cent showing in a two-man race in 1964.

We kicked off the Wisconsin campaign in Milwaukee, on a night so cold and snowy that those of us from Alabama couldn't understand why everything didn't just shut down. To the people of Wisconsin, of course, it was just another cold day. I arrived at the auditorium early and was received graciously by the Milwaukee policemen detached for the meeting. About fifteen or twenty minutes before I was scheduled to start talking, I asked one of our local organizers how the crowd looked.

"Not too good. About five hundred—maybe seven hundred. But they are still coming in."

The late arrivals made all the difference. I looked out the side windows and saw the streets filled with people getting out of cars and heading toward the auditorium. By the time I was introduced, the place was overflowing and a large number had to be turned away.

It was an inspiring reception, made especially unusual by the absence of hecklers. It encouraged me to intensify my efforts in the state, and I told my aides to arrange for more meetings, in other cities. We went on to Racine, Sheboygan, Eau Claire, Marshfield, Green Bay, La Crosse, and a number of other cities. I would have gone into many other counties in Wisconsin, but we were limited by the availability of suitable auditoriums on the dates we had open.

It is curious that I ran first in every place I visited and second in the areas I didn't get to visit. I remember the tremendous crowd that turned out in Racine. There was a little heckling, but the reception was so warm and overwhelming that it made me regret not having given Wisconsin an earlier and bigger place in my campaign planning. George McGovern had been organized there for over a year, and some thirty thousand young people were working for him all over the state, right down to the precinct level. My organization couldn't begin to compare with McGovern's, yet I managed to surprise all the so-called experts and the pollsters by running second. I am convinced it would have been a nip-and-tuck race if I had gone in earlier, right after the Florida campaign. I learned that when the people of a given area have the chance to see and hear me on TV and on the radio and meet me in person, they get a different image from the one painted by the media.

Not that I claim to have any special charisma. As a matter of fact, I am the first to recognize my failings as a TV charmer. But I console myself by reflecting that in all likelihood neither George Washington nor Abraham Lincoln would have come over too well on modern TV, with its premium on a handsome appearance, a good "image," and a melodious voice. I believe firmly that the American people are a lot less gullible than Madison Avenue takes them for and are quite capable of distinguishing between what is gilded and what is real.

Curiously, some of the experts reached that same conclusion. In the 1972 campaign, we did all our television from a studio in Alabama, and one of the networks that produced a documentary on the effectiveness of TV in nationwide campaigns reached the painful conclusion that the most effective use of television had been that of George C. Wallace of Alabama.

Ours was simple stuff, with few frills. I just sat in front of the cameras and talked directly to the people about the issues. I recall seeing some of the sophisticated TV jobs done by the advertising experts and used to wonder about our approach. Cornelia watched a few of them, then exclaimed, "My goodness, we don't have anything that big. They are really dressy. But I get the impression that it's all too artificial."

Cornelia has excellent political intuition, and I think she hit the target right in the center. People want you to talk to them. They are not interested in beautiful scenery or backdrops or elaborate productions. They don't care about seeing you with a meditative expression—they would rather know what you are meditating about. Anything artificial or contrived just turns them off.

They even like to see a few errors—the ones that humanize a candidate. I remember bobbling a few lines, then saying that I probably ought to do the tape over until I got it down pat. But Cornelia checked me.

"What's wrong with that? It shows you're human. Certainly

your long experience in speaking in public gives you an edge over others who don't have so much experience. But you're a human being, and human beings make mistakes. You make mistakes and you bobble. But I prefer to see that, because it's real."

People look for sincerity, and if that sincerity is not genuine, the viewers will know it. They don't expect a candidate to be a Greek god, just well dressed and well groomed. Tom Dewey was sleek of speech and of mustache, but he went down to defeat at the hands of a straight-talking, folksy Harry Truman.

Although, judging from recent events, perhaps mustaches are "in" again in politics.

THE LORD IS MY SHEPHERD

To be poised against fatality, to meet adverse conditions gracefully, is more than a simple endurance; it is an act of aggression, a positive triumph. —*Thomas Mann,* Death in Venice.

I lay in the ambulance, dazed but conscious. My breathing became difficult and rapid. Blood was emptying into my stomach from severed small arteries. I was bleeding to death.

A rescue unit rushed me to Holy Cross Hospital in Silver Spring, Maryland. The ambulance crew chose, wisely, a hospital with a good trauma team. When the hospital was alerted for my arrival, three members of the trauma team were having coffee in the hospital lunchroom. Nothing could have been more fortunate.

My senses were dazed, but I remember seeing and hearing people in the crowded corridor. Orders were given to clear the way for my passage. Inside the emergency room, Doctors Joseph Shanno, a vascular surgeon; John Haberlin, a general surgeon; Joseph Peabody, a chest surgeon; and Herman Magazini were waiting.

There was little time for the doctors to make an evaluation. My pulse was very rapid and my blood pressure had dropped sharply. Almost immediately, they cut into me to stop the internal bleeding. One doctor, himself a patient, removed the intravenous tubes from his body and came to surgery to help.

Shortly after I arrived at Holy Cross, a helicopter landed to transfer me to Walter Reed Hospital. Because my condition was delicate, Sister Helen Marie would not let them move me.

For the next forty-eight hours I fought to live.

Soon after the shooting, the hospital was besieged by more than two hundred representatives of TV, radio, newspapers, and magazines. The lobby was jammed with people. TV crews wheeled huge cameras, set up scores of floodlights and endless yards of electric cable. The hospital became a bedlam of scurrying newsmen, police officers, visitors, Secret Service men, members of my staff, members of my family, and hospital personnel.

Throughout the crisis, the hospital employees and physicians somehow managed to keep the hospital functioning. They were true professionals.

Bomb threats were not long in coming. Army bomb squads were sent from Fort Meade, Maryland, to handle any possible bomb emergencies.

Telephone communications were jammed with in-house, incoming, and outgoing phone calls. New lines and extra phones were installed to handle the added traffic.

The hospital's message center was swamped with tons of mail, floral arrangements, and visitors. Holy Cross handled crisis after crisis without panic. The employees, administration, and physicians cannot be praised enough. They all did a magnificent job.

I asked Sister Marie how they had managed to solve so many problems. She answered, "We could not have done it alone, Governor. God was our real support!"

Cornelia stayed cool under tremendous pressure. In addition to being my main human support, she handled a host of other things competently. She went on television to tell my supporters I was still in the fight. Many of my advisers were afraid she could not handle the press. They were wrong. Her charm and intelligence made a deep impression.

Her optimism never faltered in the critical days after I was shot. She believed, and made me believe, I was going to live. If I was depressed, she would tell me to "snap out of it." Like an army top kick she would say, "You are a lucky man and your work has just begun." She would scold me if I became even slightly resentful. There was no place for pity.

Her encouragement sounded like a tough football coach's pregame fight talk to his players. There were no soft words, but there was love and attention.

My spirits got a real boost when I learned I had won the primaries in Michigan and Maryland. I needed this kind of shot in the arm after Laurel. God willing, I would go to the Democratic Convention in Miami.

Governor Mandel of Maryland, Senator Humphrey, and Mrs. McGovern came to the hospital after I was shot. I regret that I was too sick to see them. On one of those bad days, there was a knock on my door. It opened, and there stood Glen Curlee. He smiled and said, "Greetings, Your Excellency. How are you feeling?"

I answered in a weak voice, "I don't feel so good, brother Glen."

"Well, you're not supposed to feel good. You're supposed to be dead."

"What do you mean, dead?" I asked, a bit jolted by his remark.

"Some damn fellow tried to kill you. Haven't you heard about it?"

"Oh, you mean that fellow." I wasn't making much sense.

"Yes." Glen sat down before he continued. "He didn't quite do it, did he?"

"He sure did a pretty good job of it, if you ask me." I raised my voice slightly.

"Where do you hurt?" Glen asked.

"In my side."

"Why, heck, if you were out in the wind, it would blow clean through you," he remarked.

"You're sure a sympathetic fellow," I commented.

"Now, don't go and feel sorry for yourself. The Lord has been good to you, George. Most folks aren't that lucky." His words were firm.

"I am thankful, Glen. I know the Lord made the difference this round. He may have had a little help from the doctors and nurses—but God saved me for something."

Then I added, "Glen, do you think I'm going to make it?"

"There's no question about that, Governor. You have done proved that. You're still alive, aren't you?" Then he grabbed me gently and said, "Of course you're going to make it, pardner."

Glen didn't stay long that first visit. But how glad I was to see him!

I stayed in intensive care for several weeks. When I was stronger, the doctors removed the bullet lodged near my spine.

In pictures taken several days after I was shot, I appear less worn and wan than I did six weeks later. My wounds became infected, and I lost weight during my seven weeks in the hospital.

I received a host of visitors whom I shall always remember and deeply appreciate for their concern and kindness for people: President Richard Nixon; Vice President Spiro Agnew; Senator and Mrs. Strom Thurmond; Senator and Mrs. Ted Kennedy; Senators Henry Jackson and Ed Muskie; Former Governors Edmond Brown of California and John West of South Carolina; Congressman Wilbur Mills; the two American Party candidates, Messrs. Schmitz and Anderson; Mrs. Ethel Kennedy; Sander Vanocur; Larry Spivak; and David Dick. We talked very little politics, although Senator McGovern told me that he had the nomination sewed up.

Representative Shirley Chisholm came to see me. We discussed the coming Democratic Convention, but mostly we talked about our faith in Jesus Christ. We prayed together, and I was deeply touched by her visit. I noticed there were tears in her eyes when she left. They were tears of love and compassion for another's suffering. God bless her!

After I left intensive care, I began physical therapy under the supervision of Dr. Duke. I was put on a tilt board to prevent blood-circulation problems. Paraplegics are prone to circulatory troubles if they do not get exercise. The tilt board was less taxing than using the parallel bars. I would walk the parallel bars on my hands from one end of the room to the other. At first I was too weak to turn around and needed an attendant to help me. I have come a long way since then. Today I have more arm and shoulder strength than at any time in my life.

During my first days in therapy, the doctors said they were getting me ready for the convention. I had doubts about making it, but I trained all the time to go to Miami.

I got in a great deal of wheelchair mileage. Sometimes my legs would bump some object and I would tell my nurse jokingly, "You know, I felt that clear up to my knees." Of course, I felt nothing.

Meeting with other paraplegics and sharing their experiences gave me more faith in what I could do. Unless one is crippled, he has little understanding of the problems of the physically handicapped.

I never really hated anyone before I was shot—not even my most critical political foes. After the shooting, I realize more than ever the futility of hate and resentfulness, and the frailty of people.

I believe in God and a life after death. We should be prepared to leave this life at any time. My brush with death has made me a more thoughtful man.

Many people ask me if I am bitter at Bremer. I can honestly say I am not. I have forgiven him, and I hope he has sought God's forgiveness.

Not being able to walk does not make me bitter. I wish I could walk, but I am resigned to what has happened. I regard myself as a truly fortunate man. Hate is a self-destructive emotion. To serve my family, state, and country, I must be free of rancor.

Those long hours in bed gave me time to think and reflect, to separate the gold from the dross. I thought about my father and mother saying grace before each meal. We were taught to thank God for our blessings, meager as they might seem in these affluent times. Bible study was a family affair. My grandfather said four books helped shape our country's destiny: the Bible, Shakespeare, *Pilgrim's Progress,* and Blackstone. The wisdom and spirit of our founding fathers came from those works.

I remembered that it was in Clio that I came to know and accept Jesus Christ as my personal savior. An itinerant fire-and-brimstone preacher, the Reverend Daniel Langingham, taught us that faith bridged the seen and the unseen. We were taught to place our problems in God's hands, for His will to be done.

Before each bombing mission in the Pacific, I attended religious service. I prayed to God to bring us home safely. They were the selfish prayers of a young man at war. Faith in God gave us strength to face combat.

While in intensive care, I received a letter from a nine-year-old girl. Stephanie was seriously ill. She wrote that she prayed for me and wanted to vote for me when she was old enough. I went to see her later to thank her for her prayers and to promise to keep in touch with her.

The day I left intensive care, a thin little old lady reached her hand out to me. "Governor," she said, "I have wanted to shake your hand. I want to tell you I am your supporter." I felt humble and thankful.

One day I was reading the Bible and came across a verse in St. Matthew: "Whosoever will be the chief among you, let him be your servant." I resolved that in the future I would do my best to be a worthy servant.

The hospital offered a mass for me on the day of my departure for Miami. During the mass, I read the twenty-third Psalm. David's words of comfort and faith, written three thousand years ago, are as meaningful now as then. This Psalm has put to rest more griefs than all of man's philosophies.

Sister Helen Marie, the administration, physicians, and employees gave me a farewell dinner. After the meal I was wheeled to a car, with the corridors lined with people waving and calling good-by.

I got into the car with Secret Service men. Sister Helen Marie and Sister Marita leaned in the back window to kiss me good-by. We drove to Andrews Air Force Base to fly to Miami in a plane thoughtfully provided by President Nixon. The plane was the same type used to evacuate the wounded from Vietnam. I lay on the stretcher most of the flight, sitting up only occasionally.

With me were Cornelia, Peggy, George, Jr., and Lee. Aboard were doctors and nurses to care for me if needed. I was still far from recovered.

The flight was uneventful. I looked out the window and tried to relax. I recalled my doubts about being able to make the long trip to Miami. My doctors insisted I could do it. They thought it would be good for my morale to attend the convention.

I was going to Miami because I was still a candidate and because my delegates needed my support. Perhaps a bit optimistically, I hoped to steer the platform away from McGovern's radicals and ultraliberals. But I had little expectation of influencing the delegates to move toward the center and moderation.

The newsmen were considerate of me on the flight. They did their best not to tax me with too many questions.

We made a brief stop in Montgomery, Alabama. As the plane neared the airport, I could see hundreds of cars parked parallel to the highway. I was anxious and nervous as the plane landed.

I made a speech, short and televised nationally. The weather was hot and muggy. I was afraid I might become emotional and break down. There were many old and familiar faces in the audience. But I was home, and I had no trouble talking to home folks.

The short stop gave me confidence about my appearance in Miami. I held up, as Cornelia had told me I would.

We took off for Miami. A crowd met us at the Miami airport. Among the dignitaries who received me were Miami's former mayor Chuck Hall, Governor Reuben Askew, and members of the press.

It soon became apparent to party regulars and moderates that the Democratic Party was in the hands of dedicated amateurs. Most of them were not qualified to be elected dogcatcher in their home precincts. The stage was set for McGovern's nomination.

After watching the side show, I later wondered why the masterminds of the Watergate burglary found the break-in necessary or even useful. McGovern never posed the slightest threat to Nixon in November.

I met with my delegates to draw up planks to help the Democratic Party win in November. Our minority report did not influence the convention. But it is on record for history.

McGovern's nomination was a *fait accompli*. But how he gained control of the delegates at the state conventions is interesting. Delegates to the Democratic National Convention are elected at state conventions. McGovern's partisans dominated these state conventions to elect delegates loyal to their candidate. The average American does not vote at these political conventions. McGovernites arrived in Miami with sufficient delegate strength to win the nomination.

Mississippi, which gave me an overwhelming popular vote in 1968, elected delegates pledged to Senator McGovern and Representative Shirley Chisholm. They are two fine people personally, but politically incompatible with the majority of Mississippi voters. In Miami I did not receive a single vote from the Mississippi delegation.

The same was true of Arkansas.

In Tennessee I carried every county in the 1972 primary. The state had gone to me by popular vote. But the state convention sent delegates for the most part pledged to McGovern.

Tennessee law requires its delegates to vote on the first ballot for the winner of the primary. Some delegates from Tennessee came to my room in Miami to ask me to release them. I refused, of course.

Reformers in the Democratic Party were crying before the 1972 primaries to let the people speak. Such high-sounding phrases as "participatory democracy," "affirmative action," "get involved," were shouted from within the party. But the moment the people did not vote the way the Democratic Party hierarchy wished them to vote, they came up with the idea that primaries are too costly and cumbersome.

Is there a better way for people to become involved than the presidential primary? I believe in trusting the people. Let the people go to the polls and vote for their favorite candidate. Then the delegates should support the winner and runner-ups on some proportional basis, in some equitable way. But let the people speak.

I am willing to take my chances with the people. If they want to reject me and my ideas, they have a perfect right to do so. It is appalling that the Democratic reformers who cried, "Let the people speak," are the same ones now asking to end the presidential primaries.

Eliminate the state primaries and you will increase the distrust of people in government. After Watergate, we need to restore confidence in the democratic way of life. I want to hear what the people say.

The Democratic Party hierarchy is really afraid that the wrong candidate will win the primaries. They fear the great and growing distrust of the American people. The average citizen is sick and tired of being manipulated by pseudo-intellectual bureaucrats who have helped destroy much of our freedom and civil rights.

Between visits from my delegates and the press, I watched the political circus. I was saddened when I saw Senator McGovern attempt to speak to a group of chanting radicals. The hippies kept up rhythmic chants, "Marijuana yes, Vietnam no." He tried to talk, but they ignored him and continued doing their "thing." Sadly amusing was the spectacle of delegates so fat they could hardly walk, but who demanded more relief.

I had a private visit from a group of Democratic governors. They were concerned about the radical image of McGovern. They were genuinely worried. I was asked by them, "Under what conditions would you run with Senator McGovern?" I told them his platform could not win in November, and I could never associate myself with his radical views. I said it would be impossible for us to get together on major issues and policies, foreign and domestic. They knew that McGovern would win the nomination but would lose the election.

My speech followed the keynote address of Governor Reuben Askew of Florida. I had to wait in a hot room without air conditioning. I feared that in my weak condition I might faint. An hour and a half later, I was called to the stage.

I had some misgivings about my speech. It would have to be made extemporaneously from notes. I was carried to the podium by Alabama police and Secret Service men, as the ramp built for me did not fit my wheelchair. Once on the podium, I wheeled myself to the microphone. I received a standing ovation. It was not unanimous. One state delegation remained seated—their rudeness, not mine.

It was a generous gesture, allowing me to address the convention. More than a tribute to me, it was a tribute to the millions of voters who supported me across the country. I spoke for them and to help the Democratic Party win in November.

I mentioned my earlier showing in Florida, saying that the people were not supporting Wallace so much as they were cynical of existing government, frustrated with the politicians who had proved themselves incapable of understanding or solving the basic problems confronting the American people. I charged that the two major parties "had paid attention to the noisemakers, to the exotic, ignoring the average citizen who works each day for a living and pays the taxes that hold the country together."

I reminded them that the Democratic platform called for tax reform—an issue I had hit hard in the 1968 campaign, charging that the income tax was regressive and that the "average citizen paid through the nose while the tax-free foundations went scot free." I said the minority plank would call not only for tax reform but for tax relief.

I took a strong swipe at the suffocating bureaucracy in Washington. "When we governors go to Washington and visit with one another, we whisper in each other's ears and ask, 'What do all of them do?'—the hundreds of thousands of bureaucrats who draw twenty-five to forty thousand dollars a year of the working man's money."

I talked about foreign aid. I mentioned how America had consistently been spat upon by countries that had received billions of our dollars, how we had been branded imperialist aggressors, how we had been voted against in the United Nations. I said the minority plank would speak up strongly against sending hard-earned tax money to our enemies.

I brought up the subject of welfare, saying that there is no quarrel with the idea of helping the elderly and the blind and the maimed, but that welfare programs had simply gotten out of hand, with 15–25 per cent of the persons on welfare rolls being completely ineligible. On the subject of law and order, I charged that thugs had taken over the streets of every large city in the nation, making it impossible for the average citizen to leave his home for fear of being mugged or assaulted. I expressed the hope that the next President of the United States would go on record as being for "the enforcement of the law. . . . and turning those streets back to the average man and woman, who are entitled to be able to walk in safety" wherever they live or visit.

I warned the convention that no party could win the presidency by supporting cuts in defense forces. I expressed my belief in quality education for every child and youth in the country regardless of race or color, and I charged that quality education was being impeded by "the senseless, asinine busing of little school children to achieve racial balance." I warned that "any party that doesn't confront this issue, and confront it in the right manner, is going to be in jeopardy."

It was a relatively short speech, and it was followed by polite applause.

My doctors discovered after we returned to our Miami hotel that I had a serious pocket of infection. My blood count was alarming. More surgery was needed. Before I was completely recovered, I had about eight operations.

My campaign ended informally in Laurel. It ended formally in Miami.

WITH MALICE TOWARD NONE

"Not until I went into the churches of America and heard her pulpits flame with righteousness, did I understand the secret of her genius and power. America is great because America is good . . . and if America ever ceases to be good . . . America will cease to be great." —Count Alexis de Tocqueville.

While irrigating my open wound in Miami, Dr. George Truagh discovered a new pocket of infection inside my abdomen, as mentioned in the previous chapter. New surgery was required immediately.

I was flown to Birmingham to enter the Spain Rehabilitation Center. The operation was performed soon after I arrived. Before I had recovered from surgery, a new operation was ordered by my doctors.

Regulations at Spain Hospital do not allow members of the patient's family to stay in the room with him. Cornelia insisted on being with me constantly. She did not want me to be alone when I was depressed from pain and concerned about the prospect of additional surgery. Cornelia prevailed. Hospital rules were relaxed and a cot was placed in my room for Cornelia. Her presence lifted my sagging morale.

As quickly as I could, I took physical therapy to regain my strength. Weight lifting and workouts on parallel bars were part of my therapy. Soon I was able to do many things without help.

Despite my obvious physical improvement, I did not regain my lost weight, and I had little appetite. Home furloughs got me away from hospital routine and institutional cooking. The mansion atmosphere did wonders. I began to gain weight, and my appetite returned.

The American Independent Party held its national convention

while I was hospitalized. There were plans under way to draft me as its presidential standard-bearer in 1972. I had strict orders to abstain from any politicking until I was completely well. With open wounds and drainage tubes, I was hardly ready for the rigors of a presidential campaign. I cabled party leaders that I would not be a candidate under any circumstances.

The cable had little effect on my supporters. It was necessary to talk with the delegates by telephone from my hospital bed. My decision not to run was accepted graciously after they learned of my true condition.

Slightly more than three months after I was shot in Laurel, I celebrated my fifty-third birthday, in the governor's office. I had started the long road back to full recovery.

President Nixon telephoned me several times while I was in the hospital. He suggested I take baths in a salt-water pool. Later he sent me a film on the life of Franklin D. Roosevelt. We did not talk politics in our conversations.

Senator McGovern also telephoned me three times during the presidential campaign. He wanted my endorsement for the presidency. In one of our conversations, he asked, "Governor, how can I get the support you got in the spring primaries? I have run across your backers in Pennsylvania, Ohio, Illinois, Michigan, and Indiana. They tell me that without your endorsement I can't win."

I thanked him and said, "George, I can tell you only what I told the people. They evidently liked my views enough to vote for me. After all, politics is politics—people hunting votes."

It was already too late for him to alter his political course. He was a captive of the radical wing of the Democratic Party.

He called later to ask me to endorse him before a national press conference. He persisted in believing I could swing the election to him. I did not believe any one man could change the outcome in November. Senator McGovern made no offers to me in exchange for my support. I closed our conversation by telling him I had stayed out of the campaign on doctors' orders and I had made no public statement supporting any candidate. I did promise to call him if I changed my mind.

The night before the election, he called again. "Governor, you will probably vote early. I would appreciate it if you would tell the press you have voted the Democratic ticket. I believe it is not too late to win." I made no promise. Senator McGovern did not press me, only requested.

In the morning I went to the polls to cast my ballot. I was not active in general-election politics in 1972.

Nixon's victory was an unprecedented landslide. But in the moment of his greatest triumph a scandal was brewing that would unseat him from office; Watergate would soon shock the nation.

Among other things, Watergate disclosed that the Committee to Re-Elect the President gave four hundred thousand dollars to my political opponent to defeat me in Alabama's 1970 gubernatorial campaign. Committee strategists were obviously looking ahead to the 1972 presidential campaign. National Republicans wanted me out of the way politically. Even some Democrats would have agreed that it would be a good thing to "pull the rug out from under Wallace."

President Nixon's notorious "enemies list" included my name. The President had ordered the IRS to bring my file to him personally. Soon afterward, hordes of IRS agents descended to Montgomery to harass me, my family, and my supporters. Ironically, the IRS discovered they owed me money—a disclosure that pleased me immensely.

This sordid use of our tax-collecting apparatus is not in keeping with the American system of justice. Americans were shocked to learn that an agency of the government was used by an incumbent to persecute political enemies. No one likes a Gestapo.

I have never harassed a single state employee because of his personal views. If you want to make political enemies fast, start persecuting little people. If I conduct myself fairly to all state employees, those who oppose me may someday become my supporters.

Watergate was the symptom, not the disease. Naked power unchecked by moral restraint was the cause. Ends had become more important than the means. Situation ethics were substituted for absolute values. Personal accountability was subordinated to political expediency. Win was the only name of the game.

The time was ripe for deep soul-searching in our nation.

I did not hear from President Nixon again until I was elected chairman of the Southern Governors Conference in September of 1972. He asked about my health and congratulated me.

My election was a generous act on the part of the governors from my region. Governor West of South Carolina, who was scheduled to be the chairman, declined in my favor. He was the outgoing governor of South Carolina and, unless he ran again, he would have no chance of ever being chosen chairman. I will never forget his gallant gesture.

Shortly before we entertained some returning POWs in the mansion, President Nixon telephoned again. He asked me to convey his deep appreciation to the servicemen and their families for their sacrifices during the Vietnam War. President Nixon later hosted the same servicemen in the White House.

When President Nixon was ill at San Clemente, I sent him a personal message, along with some flowers. Although I had not approved of everything he had done, I felt compassion for him when he was down. Perhaps more than before I was shot, I have come to appreciate the quality of mercy. I regretted it was necessary to remove a President from office.

I later received a call from the ex-President to thank me for my message and flowers. My troopers at first thought it was a hoax call. They cleared the call with President Nixon before we spoke. His voice sounded sad when he said, "I just wanted to thank you and Cornelia for your concern for me when I was ill."

"Mr. President," I told him, "I want to apologize for not telephoning you when you were sick. I should have done it, but I feared I might be intruding. Please forgive me."

We chatted a short while. Before I finished talking, I said, "Your accomplishments will be remembered in the long view of history. Keep your chin up and God bless you." He closed by saying, "If you and your lovely wife are ever in California, please come and see me." At Christmastime I received a handwritten card from him.

Friends of mine contacted the Free Chinese Government in Taiwan. They were anxious to help me in any way possible. They recommended Dr. Chu, the famed acupuncturist of New York City. Dr. Chu was contacted and agreed to visit me in Montgomery.

I was ready for any treatment that would ease the pain. Dr.

Chu was a jovial and sympathetic person. His medical credentials were impeccable. I liked him immediately.

When he arrived in Montgomery I was depressed about my health. My personal physicians were dubious about acupuncture treatments. Reluctantly, they permitted Dr. Chu to treat me.

After Dr. Chu had completed his examination, my doctors ordered him to treat me for pain only. There ensued a clash between the established and the new.

Dr. Chu protested. "I know what I am doing. Reviewing the governor's medical record, I have hope of regeneration in his case, and this hope is sustained by an examination of his partially injured spinal cord. The damaged part can be taken over by the undamaged part, according to neurophysiological knowledge. Acupuncture can not only stop the pain, I believe there is hope that the governor may walk."

He was confident and optimistic. His report was the kind of cautious tonic I needed. To pacify the understandably angered doctor, I intervened. "Why not treat just the pain this time, Dr. Chu? If you succeed, then surely no one will be able to object to you treating my physical problems next time." Dr. Chu generously accepted the compromise.

I looked forward to his weekly visits, and we became good friends. We discussed China and the history of acupuncture. Our exchanges on many subjects were stimulating to me. He confessed he enjoyed the change from New York to Montgomery.

After nearly a year of acupuncture, I had improved visibly. My legs had more color and there was temperature. There was volume and muscle tone for the first time since I was shot. My doctors verified this, but countered with the objection, "Any form of stimulation would have done the same thing."

I am unable to say categorically that acupuncture helped. As a non-medical layman, I lack the knowledge to take sides in the controversy. Unfortunately, more medical differences developed between my physicians and Dr. Chu, and the treatments were suspended.

On becoming a paraplegic, I had to change many things in my life. It takes longer for me to get in and out of bed and to go to the bathroom. My bathroom has special wall bars for me to hold on to when I bathe and shave. Before I was shot I could shower and shave in a few minutes. Paraplegics take a little longer.

I don't get up as early, because I stay up late at night. The evenings I use for returning telephone calls, dictating letters, and reading. Some state business can be done by telephone. It saves many department heads long trips to Montgomery.

After I dress in the morning, I take my physical exercises. I start in the standing box, for one hour or more. Next come the parallel bars, on which I move forward and backward rapidly; this exercise I do with my braces on. Then I lift one hundred-pound weights over my head no less than fifty times. My shoulders and arms are stronger now than when I boxed thirty-five years ago.

During my standing exercises I can use the telephone. In the therapy room I have fewer interruptions than I do in the office. At the office I am exposed to a constant flow of people wishing to chat and shake hands.

I usually leave for the office at noon, returning around seven in the evening. When possible, I like to reserve the evenings for the family. Unless we have a banquet or a state function, I seldom go out in the evening.

I have not reduced my out-of-state travel, although I do find that I travel less in Alabama. If I become lazy, Cornelia will insist on getting me dressed to go for a drive in the country. The weekends are reserved for the family and visits of old friends.

It was during my stay in the Spain rehab hospital that I learned to understand the problems paraplegics and quadriplegics face when they return home. Most of their families must work and can look after them only on the side. This situation creates anguish for the paraplegic and financial stresses for the family.

The mental capacity of paraplegics and quadriplegics is not impaired. Once they have adjusted to their physical limitations, they become useful citizens again. They are too valuable a human resource to be forgotten and neglected. While in the hospital, I made up my mind to help paraplegics and other severely crippled people in my state.

I have sponsored a program to benefit the quadriplegic/paraplegic and his family. It includes medical assistance, counseling, job procurement, and financial aid to the family.

My greatest satisfaction as a public servant comes from creating social programs that help people to help themselves. There are other rewards in public service; but for me nothing equals the satisfaction derived from building schools, hospitals, roads, public facilities, and parks. These things outlive petty politics.

And what about my feelings toward the man who caused me all this suffering, Arthur Bremer? I would certainly be deceiving myself as well as others if I were to state flatly that I have known no bitterness or resentment. It has been no easy task to reconcile or resign myself to the life of a paraplegic, just as it has been no easy task to dig deep into my Christian faith to forgive the culprit.

Nevertheless, I have come a long way toward this goal. I defy anyone who has gone through what I have gone through to refrain from raising an occasional cry to heaven and asking, "Why did this have to happen to me?" But when a man has had as much time as I have for reflection, he begins to get a faint insight into the mysterious workings of God's will—to understand how insignificant he and his own personality are in the cosmic scheme of things. I accept—with normal human petulance—the fact that what happened was in all likelihood God's incomprehensible way of testing my faith and my forbearance, no matter how often I may wonder wryly if I was really worth all the attention. My thoughts go back to the thousands of Christian martyrs whose suffering exceeded my own, and I achieve a condition satisfactorily close to peace with myself and my Maker.

As for Bremer, I have tried sincerely to forgive the man, and I honestly believe I have done so—although I continue to hate the crime he committed. There is little left of rancor, although there are plenty of lingering questions and doubts about his motivations. When I think of him now, my thoughts are mostly centered on the mystery surrounding the attack and on the contradictions between what he appears to be and what I believe he may really be.

I wonder, for example, where he got the money to stalk me across so many states, to rent limousines, buy a car, frequent good eating places, and stay at the Waldorf-Astoria in New York. This is hardly the lifestyle one would expect of a part-time bus boy.

After I was shot, an internationally known detective remarked,

"To solve the shooting of Governor Wallace, the motive must be found." The motive has not been found. Although I have no proof on which to base any accusation against any group, it is difficult for me to accept the theory that Bremer was a "loner." The contradictions indicate that it went deeper than that.

I have read Bremer's diary, and something about it does not ring true. It has a contrived tone to it, as though it were deliberately written to throw off inquiry into a possible conspiracy. Is it a mere coincidence that in a country where few people keep diaries any more, just about all the political assassins have been "Dear Diary" addicts?

Bremer's trip to Canada strikes me as a decoy, and I doubt whether Nixon ever was Bremer's target. But I am convinced that I was—right from the day he started working as a volunteer in my Wisconsin campaign organization, and until he nailed me in Laurel.

His diary is a strange combination of flashes of rather brilliant prose mixed with phrases even an illiterate would be ashamed of. Reading it, one gets the feeling that it was written by an educated man—but an educated man trying to give an impression of a mediocre and emotionally disturbed mind. It is full of inconsistencies. Easy words are incorrectly spelled, while difficult words are spelled perfectly. He gives five or six different spellings for the words "surprise" and "barricade." Yet he uses and spells precisely the seldom employed word "gargoyle." Are we really to believe that he is a low-intellect high school dropout?

We know little about him. In late March of 1972 he worked in Milwaukee as a volunteer in my primary campaign. He is reported as being hard-working and extremely punctual, somewhat aloof, but willing to do any work assigned to him. He usually wore blue jeans and a tight T-shirt; his hair was slightly long. By the time he reached Maryland, his clothing style had changed. When he shot me he was wearing a neat blue blazer and slacks—rather like a movie version of Joe College in the '40s.

He presented himself to Grey Hodges as an amateur photographer, saying he wanted to get a close shot of me. He certainly did! Although he didn't mix much with the other campaign workers, he was very chummy with the telephone receptionist at the Milwaukee Holiday Inn. This very receptionist was later caught monitoring our telephone calls, and as a precaution she was removed from the job. I don't know whether there was any foundation for the subsequent comment that she had connections with certain left-wing organizations.

Bremer drove up in front of the Holiday Inn one night in a late-model Lincoln Continental. Grey Hodges recalls the driver as being dark and strangely tense. Bremer jumped out and excitedly asked Hodges, "Has the governor arrived?" When Hodges replied in the negative, Bremer motioned with his hand to the driver, and the Lincoln pulled away. Hodges was asking himself what this semi-hippie type was doing in such a fancy car, and he put the question to Bremer, "Hey, fellow, what is a hippie like you doing in a limousine?"

Bremer replied, "Oh, I just got a ride with him. Never saw the man before." Hodges dismissed the incident and never mentioned it until after the shooting.

It could all be nothing more than coincidence, but it makes one wonder—about this, as well as about other assassinations and attempts at assassination. There are too many gnawing questions surrounding the death of the Kennedy brothers, the killing of Martin Luther King, and the attempt on my life. I think it would be proper for Congress to conduct a search for new evidence and new light in all these cases.

In recent years, state governors have become more concerned about big government swallowing up state and local government. Today there is a lot of talk about local responsibility, local government. Even the dishonored term "states' rights" is used.

I am gratified to see that states that created the federal union are finally asserting their constitutional rights. Our federal Constitution would never have been ratified by the states without the inclusion of the first ten amendments, which the Supreme Court has so systematically violated.

When the states accept federal funding for state projects, it is merely the taxpayers' money being returned to them. No government ever makes money. American productivity keeps our government going.

I look forward to the contacts each year at the governors conference. We have an opportunity to exchange ideas, and I have picked up many useful ideas on state government from these exchanges.

I remember a conference I attended back in the 1960s. When it came time to name the host state for the following year's conference, I put in a bid for Alabama. I knew full well in those controversial, civil-rights years that Alabama would be passed over. In jest I told the governors, "I would like to invite you governors to Alabama. You have given me so much advice on how to run my state, you might just be able to solve some of our problems."

The heartiest laugh came from a governor who had previously sent me a stiff cable during the civil-rights period. I had replied to his cable: "You have enough problems in your own state to keep you busy, and you don't seem to be doing such a good job in solving them. Mind your own business."

I don't get cables like that any more. But if I did I have the maturity just to ignore them.

When Mrs. Liuzzo was tragically killed in Alabama, I received a cable from some official in Alaska blaming me for the senseless murder. In anger I wired back, "I hold you personally responsible for the earthquake in Alaska. By running off at the mouth you set off the earth tremors."

Vice-President Johnson attended the governors conference in 1963. After the traditional first dance had ended, a drunken Dallas newsman walked up to him and said, "You're not my VP, Wallace is!" I was quite embarrassed and apologized for the newsman's rudeness. "Oh, forget it, George," said Johnson. "Old so-and-so never did like me. Those things just happen."

I have been acquainted personally with all our Presidents. I found President Johnson the easiest to get along with. He was a warm and friendly man, and I always felt at ease with him.

For years my political foes and the mass media have tried to stereotype me as a Southerner who dislikes people because of race. But it's a brand that won't stick. As governor, I have taken special pains to build schools for both races. Trade schools have sprung up in Alabama for all to attend. I worked and continue to work with mayors and county commissioners for a better understanding among all our citizens. We have racial peace in Alabama because the good people of both races make a sincere effort to get along with each other.

In the last gubernatorial election, I had the overwhelming support of both races. This is a matter of record.

Many newsmen accuse me of trying to change my image. Image is very important to the Madison Avenue crowd. The personality packagers live in a world of "product selling." I frankly don't care too much what journalists write. My conscience, not the mythmakers, tells me who I am.

Times have changed. Segregation in public facilities is now out of the realm of discussion, and I certainly have no intention and no desire to turn back the clock. Segregation has been outlawed by legislative and judicial action, and people have accepted these social changes, because they are basically law-abiding. Racial harmony in our region comes as no surprise to me. The two races have lived side by side for hundreds of years.

Newspapers and TV people would have it appear that I have deliberately courted black favor. In one sense they are right, because as a politician I court favor wherever I think I can find it. But I am not trying to give a face-lift to my image. The media wrote that I "dropped in" on the black mayors conference in Tuskegee. Both times I was invited by Mayor Ford of Tuskegee. The black mayors very courteously stayed another half day to hear me speak. I told them—as I have told all—that I am still opposed to big government. I pointed out that "Big Brother" government is just as much a threat to blacks as to whites. We should all unite to curtail federal power in Washington.

The pastor of the Dexter Avenue Baptist Church in Montgomery invited me to speak. It was not a civil-rights meeting but a worship service. I expressed my thanks to the pastor and to the congregation for their prayers when my condition was delicate. In order to avoid turning the meeting into a press show, I deliberately did not notify the press.

Not long ago, I attended the IOC Conference in Atlanta, where I was honored along with other southern governors for our efforts in helping the hard-core poor and unemployed. I was introduced by Mayor Ford, and the response was enthusiastic. There were many distinguished blacks in attendance, including the lieutenant governor of Colorado.

I told them I had been born in the rural South, where people of both races were, with few exceptions, poor. I had lived in a house that leaked and had no running water. My parents could not afford, in the bottom of the Depression, to buy me a Sears-catalog cowboy suit costing a dollar. I knew what it meant to do without things.

The "limousine liberals" in Washington, I said, talked one way and acted another. Most of them had never known privation in their lives. They feel guilty for being rich.

I believe those of us who have known poverty can better understand the poor than the self-flagellating liberals who were born with silver spoons in their mouths. Too much of the ultrarich concern for the poor is mere political pandering.

I remember when I was growing up as a boy in the Old South, there was a tenant farmer I used to ride with in the summer, mounted on a bale of cotton on the way to the gin. He was technically illiterate, in the sense that he lacked a formal education and had had to grub for a living right from childhood. He lived in a house with no screens, a primitive-type dwelling. He was about thirty years old at the time, and I was eleven at the most. He wore a wool hat that had somehow survived heaven knows how many winters and summers, a pair of brogans, no socks, probably no underwear, frayed overalls, and a coarse shirt.

When the mules pulled the wagon up to the gin house, we used to lie on the cotton while waiting for other wagons to move ahead. It still gives me a nostalgic feeling to recall those days.

But what impressed me most was this man's love for his country, in spite of the fact that he was certainly one of its most poverty-stricken citizens. "You know, George C.," he used to say (everybody called me George C.), "ours is the strongest country in the world. We can whup all the countries in the world put together. The United States could take them all on at one time."

This was his simplistic way of expressing his love for this country, in spite of the fact that he had nothing material and the system had not been as good to him as it should have been. He was one of thousands upon thousands who had faith that things would get better—and they did get better. Today, some of his offspring are enjoying the good life and a higher education. This man who had virtually nothing was ready to stand up for his country, in contrast with so many people today who have everything under the sun and are doing their best to destroy our democratic system.

Certainly our nation has its faults, but in our system of government is contained the mechanism for correcting them. I think the record will show that the United States has corrected more of its faults and has overcome more of its shortcomings than any other nation in all history. And I think a dispassionate evaluation of our current problems will reveal that most of them are caused and contrived by people who have somehow lost the simple, patriotic faith of our fathers. They are so intent on pointing out the motes that they have overlooked the basic beauty and wholesomeness that still prevail in our land and in our people.

If my message to my fellow citizens were to be summed up in a single phrase, it would be: "Let's Stand Up for America!"

INDEX